Washington D.C. RUNNING Guide

Washington D.C. RUNNING Guide

CITY RUNNING GUIDE SERIES

DON CARTER

BOB McCULLOUGH

Human Kinetics

Library of Congress Cataloging-in-Publication Data

Carter, Don, 1949-
   Washington, DC., running guide / Don Carter, Bob McCullough.
      p.   cm. -- (City running guide series)
   ISBN 0-88011-726-5
   1. Running--Washington Metropolitan Area--Guidebooks.
   2. Washington Metropolitan Area--Guidebooks.   I. McCullough, Bob,
   1956-   .   II. Title.   III. Series.
   GV1061.22.W37C37   1999
   917.5304'41--dc21   98-40542
                                                            CIP

ISBN: 0-88011-726-5

Acquisitions Editor: Martin Barnard; **Developmental Editor**: Kent Reel; **Assistant Editors**: Rebecca Crist and Leigh LaHood; **Copyeditor**: Bob Replinger; **Proofreader**: Myla Smith; **Graphic Designer**: Stuart Cartwright; **Graphic Artist**: Sandra Meier; **Photo Editor**: Boyd LaFoon; **Cover Designer**: Jack Davis; **Photographer (cover)**: Mae Scanlan; **Photographer (interior)**: Photos on pages xiii, xiv, and 102 © Kenneth Lee; photo on page 40 © RAM Associates; **Illustrator**: Accurate Art, Inc. and Tom Roberts; **Printer**: Versa Press

Text on page 115 provided by Kathy Freedman

Human Kinetics books are available at special discounts for bulk purchase. Special editions or book excerpts can also be created to specification. For details, contact the Special Sales Manager at Human Kinetics.

Printed in the United States of America   10   9   8   7   6   5   4   3   2   1

Human Kinetics
Web site: http://www.humankinetics.com/

United States: Human Kinetics, P.O. Box 5076, Champaign, IL 61825-5076
1-800-747-4457
e-mail: humank@hkusa.com

Canada: Human Kinetics, 475 Devonshire Road Unit 100, Windsor, ON N8Y 2L5
1-800-465-7301 (in Canada only)
e-mail: humank@hkcanada.com

Europe: Human Kinetics, P.O. Box IW14, Leeds LS16 6TR, United Kingdom
(44) 1132 781708
e-mail: humank@hkeurope.com

Australia: Human Kinetics, 57A Price Avenue, Lower Mitcham, South Australia 5062
(088) 277 1555
e-mail: humank@hkaustralia.com

New Zealand: Human Kinetics, P.O. Box 105-231, Auckland 1
(09) 523 3462
e-mail: humank@hknewz.com

CONTENTS

INTRODUCTION

Some cities seem almost designed for great downtown running but have little to offer in outlying areas. Others present pristine routes beyond their borders, but the downtown area is either too small, too congested, or too much of an urban wasteland to offer much in the way of running.

Washington offers the best of both worlds. The downtown attractions are relatively concentrated near a three- to five-mile stretch of bridges along the Potomac, with bike paths to the north and south that make it easy to extend these routes farther into Maryland or Virginia.

Beyond the downtown area, Washingtonians can choose from an array of routes that have their foundation in the area's excellent network of bike paths. These paths extend outward in all directions from the downtown area, and they cover a lot of ground. Within the downtown area they allow runners to avoid the perils of urban traffic. Beyond the city they can turn what would be an otherwise mundane run into an aesthetically pleasing athletic experience.

In many cases these bike paths are also adjacent to parks, and the fact that they tend to funnel into one another makes it easy to design a route combining two or more paths. Yet another endearing characteristic of Washington is relatively flat terrain—while the area has an abundance of routes with gently rolling hills, you'll have to look hard to do really serious hill training.

If there's a downside to all this convenience, it's a slight tendency for Washington running to get a bit homogenous beyond the downtown area. The urban variety offered by the Mall, Rock Creek Park, and Arlington National Cemetery is hard to match within such a relatively small area, but the run beyond D.C. proper tends to be a jaunt on a bike path along a meandering stream. Fortunately, the outlying areas also offer a fine array of trail-running options, from the historical ambiance of Battlefield Park and Bull Run to the naturalistic attractions of the Patuxent Wildlife Refuge.

Keeping these generalizations in mind, the best way to use this guide is to take an inside-out approach. That is, start with the downtown area, which is relatively easy to negotiate, and then work your way out in a desired direction depending on your particular running tastes. Once you start working your way out toward the Beltway, the network of interconnections that define D.C. running routes will quickly produce a variety of options.

The following sections outline transportation concerns, safety issues, and the inevitable weather considerations. Despite the fact that Beltway traffic has become the stuff of legend, it is possible to drive to most of these routes, especially if your schedule is somewhat flexible. If you're a subway type, the Metro is arguably one of the finest mass-transit systems in the country.

The combination of bike paths and tourist traffic in the downtown area tends to make D.C. a safer running city than many of its Northeast counterparts, but you should take the same precautions here that you do in any major city. As for the weather, Washington is an almost idyllically mild running city three seasons of the year—the less said about summer, the better.

TRANSPORTATION

The difficulties of driving to and from any run site in the D.C. area can be summed up in three words: Beware the Beltway. Getting around the perimeter of the Washington area is a nightmare from seven to nine in the morning and four to six in the afternoon.

The good news is that the abundance of Beltway traffic makes parts of the downtown area seem manageable by comparison. Although the bridges along the Potomac clog up during rush hour, some of the secondary highways in and out of town are surprisingly negotiable. With minimal knowledge of traffic patterns and a flexible schedule you can get to most of these runs without too much trouble.

Mass transit provides both visitors and downtown residents a pleasurable way to get from one run site to another in D.C. Complementing the easy-to-connect bridge routes and bike paths, the Metro makes it possible to move quickly and easily from one part of the city to another. In several instances routes have been designed so that you can use the Metro as one half of a longer out-and-back excursion.

Although the Metro is clean, easy to negotiate, and reasonably safe, there is one caveat for visitors. Unlike most subway systems where you simply buy a one-price-fits-all token and ride to your destination, the

Metro requires you to purchase a ticket for a specific destination and pay accordingly. To avoid overpaying, use signs posted in the station to determine the fare for your destination. You can then purchase a fare ticket for the exact amount. The ticket machines accept bills and provide change—but don't use a large bill for a small fare unless you want to carry around a lot of quarters!

WEATHER

Washington weather tends toward the mild side. With the possible exception of the West Coast cities it probably has the best three-season running climate in the country. Spring itself, of course, is a major tourist attraction, especially when the cherry blossoms come out and the tulips and azaleas bloom, but the pleasures of spring running here extend far beyond the famous runs along the Potomac. Fall is almost as nice. A colorful foliage season may not be the equal of its Northeastern neighbors, but the length and warmth of the season more than make up for whatever may be lacking in the leaf palette.

Winters in Washington are relatively mild, with daytime highs generally above freezing and storms that usually present minimal accumulations. Snowfall is not uncommon, but an inch or two at a time is far more common than a major storm. Ice is also a concern here—below-freezing temperatures at night can turn running into ice skating in sneakers until the guilty weather front passes through.

Another annoying aspect of Washington weather is mud season, which usually starts around November and goes through April, depending on the mix and frequency of rain and snow through the winter. This is the time of year when macadam bike paths become essential because the trails can turn slick and gooey, even in the downtown area.

Summer, of course, is hot and humid. From late June through the end of August midday running requires a host of precautions—thorough hydration, the search for shade, shortening up on length a bit, and so on. There is no defense, however, for the horrendous humidity, save for running early in the morning or late in the afternoon to avoid the combination of high sun and drenched air.

SAFETY

No activity is free of risk, and running is no exception. The relative abundance of year-round tourist traffic makes the popular downtown runs a bit safer here than those in most cities, and the fact that the bike paths are well traveled helps too. However, it is an unfortunate truth that no area is completely safe, and that serious attacks have occurred on the routes described in this guide. Don't let yourself be a victim; use common sense and take appropriate precautions.

The Road Runners Club of America developed an excellent set of safety guidelines for women runners that we have adapted and slightly modified for this guide. They form a solid set of "rules of the road" for both trail and road running to help make your running safer.

1. Don't wear headsets. Use your ears to be aware of your surroundings.

2. Carry coins for a phone call.

3. Run with a partner.

4. Write down or leave word of the direction of your run. Friends and family should know the particulars of your favorite running routes.

5. If you're running in an unfamiliar area, know where the phones are and the location of stores and businesses that will be open. In familiar areas, alter your route patterns occasionally.

6. Always stay alert. Don't run or exceed your capacity when excessively tired.

7. Whenever possible, avoid unpopulated areas, deserted streets, and overgrown trails. Avoid unlit areas at night, and when possible run clear of parked cars and bushes.

8. Carry ID—name, phone number, blood type, and any appropriate medical information. Avoid wearing conspicuous jewelry.

9. Ignore verbal harassment and use discretion in acknowledging strangers. Look directly at others and be observant, but keep your distance and keep moving.

10. When possible (and when it's safe to do so), run against traffic so that you can observe passing automobiles.

11. Be especially cautious about running at twilight or before dawn, and wear reflective material. In general, don't run after dark.

12. Use your intuition about a person or an area. React according to your intuition and avoid either if unsure.

13. Carry a whistle or noisemaker.

14. If possible, memorize license tags or identifying characteristics of suspicious cars or strangers.

15. Call police immediately if something happens to you or someone else, or if you notice anything out of the ordinary.

The Road Runners Club of America also compiles and distributes a free periodic bulletin, "Incidents on Area Roads, Parks and Trails," that lists recent problems encountered by runners, bicyclists, and walkers in the Washington, D.C., area. A copy can be obtained by contacting the RRCA at 1150 S. Washington Street, Suite 250, Alexandria, Virginia, 22314.

Finally, we offer two other safety caveats. First, exercise caution in crossing streets, particularly in the downtown area. There are many distractions among the monuments of Washington, and vehicles running red lights are all too common. Second, the off-road paths are heavily used by bicyclists as well as runners. Stay alert to avoid collisions.

ICON KEY

Distance Given in miles	**8.2 MILES**
Terrain	**ROAD** (asphalt, concrete) / **TRAIL** (dirt, grass)
Restrooms on course	🚻
Drinking water on course	💧
Telephone on course	☎
Scenery Icons	Capitol 🏛 Park 🌳
SCENERY RATING	rated 1 to 5 icons
HILL RATING	rated 1 hill (flat) to 5 hills (ferocious)
Start = ●	Finish = ▲ Turnaround = ↻

DOWNTOWN WASHINGTON

INTRODUCTION

Downtown Washington almost seems as if it were designed for running. Like many cities built along a river, it's possible to put together a series of routes that run from one bridge to the next, selecting distance and scenery according to whatever combination of whim and necessity seems appropriate. Unlike most cities with this basic geography, however, most of Washington's prime tourist attractions are near one another, making it easy to link them in a series of loops and routes.

Given this structure, running in downtown Washington is almost like putting together a jigsaw puzzle. Pick an attraction, park, bridge,

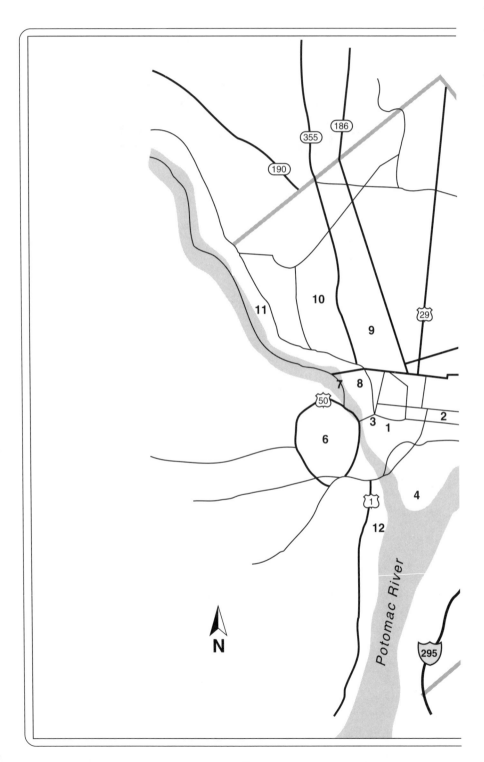

Downtown Washington

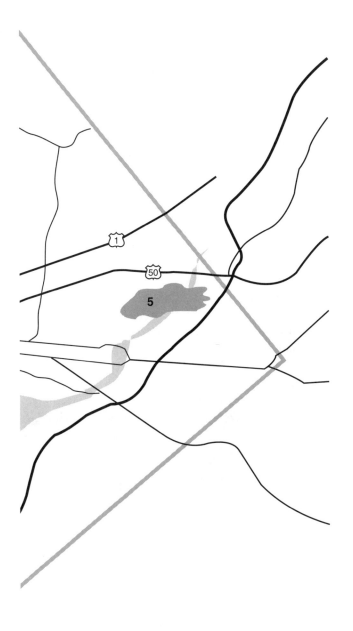

or major landmark, select the distance, weigh the scenery tradeoffs, and then lace 'em up and go. Indeed, an ultra-ambitious ultramarathoner could design a loop incorporating all of these routes, thus turning the traditional D.C.-tourist sightseeing experience into the proverbial three-hour tour. This theoretical course designer would probably replicate a good portion of the Marine Corps Marathon.

Another advantage of running in downtown Washington is the ease with which you can follow the various routes. Most are intuitive in the best running sense of the word—the directional stumbling blocks are minimal, and you can get from one to another without too much logistical fuss. Many of the trails in the downtown area are well marked, and distances are simple to gauge because the markers list the distance from one section or trail to the next.

As in most major Northeastern cities, parking and mass-transit issues are often the chief obstacles, but even in this respect Washington grades out better than most of its bustling contemporaries. The mass-transit system is convenient and easy to use. Downtown parking is easier than in most other cities, although the parking gods that live near the Potomac have their share of capricious days.

As a running city, Washington is organized inside-out, with most of the best routes clustered in a relatively small area. For example, the Tidal Basin loop is too short to be a stand-alone route, but it's easily linked to the Mall, which can be connected to one of the two Arlington Memorial Bridge routes or lower Rock Creek Park, and so on. Nearby extensions and options are either listed within each route or covered in a brief section that follows the description, depending on the size of the extension and which approach makes the most organizational sense.

TIDAL BASIN LOOP

1.8 MILES	ROAD/TRAIL	SCENERY RATING	
	🚻 💧 ☎	HILL RATING	

ACCESS

The Tidal Basin is located just northwest of the 14th Street Bridge and can be reached from numerous highways and local streets. Route 395 to the east is probably the most commonly used highway. The best option for metered and garage parking is the northwest side of the Mall between 23rd Street and 17th Street. In addition, the Park Service maintains free lots off Ohio Drive and east Basin Drive—but pay close attention to the signs for permissible parking hours.

If you're running this route from a mass-transit stop, the best bet is the Smithsonian Metro station, which puts you on the Independence Avenue side of the Mall near 12th Street. From there you can run west on Independence and head south to the Tidal Basin on either 15th Street to Raoul Wallenberg Place or on 17th Street (see map).

COURSE

Although it might seem logical to start this section with the Mall, the Tidal Basin makes more sense because of its central location. This route is the hub of downtown D.C. road running, a circular loop tucked between the Mall and East Potomac Park. It's also right between Washington's two most popular running bridges, the Arlington Memorial Bridge (known locally as the Memorial Bridge) and the George Mason Bridge (referred to as the 14th Street Bridge). In addition, it forms the backdrop for Washington's famous cherry blossoms, which encircle the basin with a spectacular pink bloom in late March and early April.

At 1.8 miles, the Tidal Basin Loop is barely long enough to be a stand-alone run, but it connects easily with the 4.8-mile Mall loop, the 3.5-mile run down to Hains Point through East Potomac Park, or the Memorial Bridge–14th Street Bridge loop.

Where you start depends on whether you're running from the Smithsonian Metro station or where you wind up parking if you're not. Anywhere near the Jefferson Memorial on the east side of the loop, for instance, makes for an ideal starting point if you're heading over to East Potomac Park. On the opposite side of the basin, you can take either Raoul Wallenberg Place or 17th Street to get to the Mall loop. The river side could also be the starting point for a bridge loop, beginning at the FDR Memorial located between the river and the Tidal Basin. Running is not allowed in the memorial, but you can walk through the open-air, fountain-filled memorial in your running clothes.

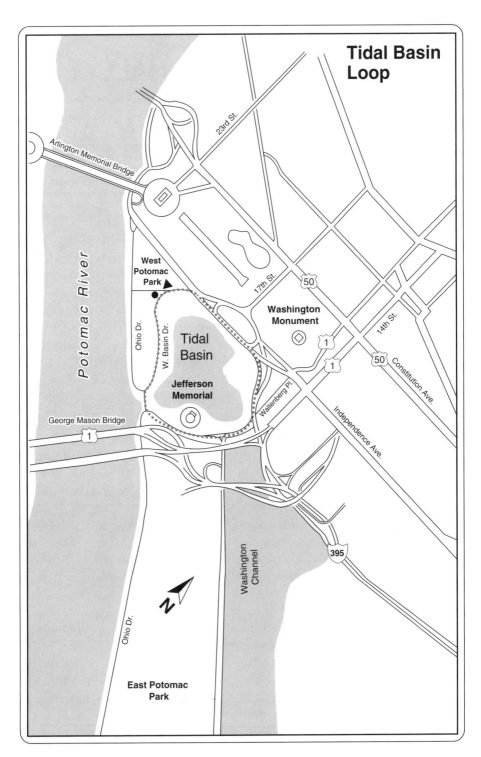

Tidal Basin Loop

Arlington Memorial Bridge

Potomac River

23rd St.

17th St.

50

West Potomac Park

Washington Monument

14th St.

Ohio Dr.

W. Basin Dr.

Tidal Basin

50

1

1

50

Constitution Ave.

Jefferson Memorial

Wallenberg Pl.

George Mason Bridge

1

Independence Ave.

395

Washington Channel

Ohio Dr.

N

East Potomac Park

INDEPENDENCE MALL

4.8- 5.2 MILES	TRAIL	SCENERY RATING					
		HILL RATING					

ACCESS

On-street, two-hour metered parking (or garage parking) for this loop can usually be found off Independence Avenue between 17th Street and 23rd; a short hunt may be required. If you're arriving by mass transit, start from the Smithsonian Metro station, which puts you on the Independence Avenue side of the Mall near 12th Street. From there you can run east or west on Independence, cross over to Constitution Avenue, or use either Madison Drive or Jefferson Drive within the Mall itself.

COURSE

The 5-mile loop around the Mall is Washington's showcase run, offering a choice of terrain, excellent scenery, a modicum of shade, and the option to add other routes in the downtown area. This is the nation's ultimate tourist loop, offering the opportunity to take in most of the downtown attractions in a single shot.

The Mall loop runs up and down Constitution Avenue and Independence Avenue. If you're on the park-and-run plan, starting from the Constitution Avenue side of the mall between 23rd and 17th Streets makes sense for several reasons. It puts Capitol Hill in the middle of the route and balances the scenery nicely, providing a view of the Washington Monument at the beginning along with a sidelong glance at the White House, then finishing with breathtaking greenery as you begin your final kick past the Lincoln Memorial.

Within the loop, you can run either on the wide crushed-gravel trails within the Mall or along the sidewalks around the perimeter. In general, the inner trails are better—they make street crossings easier and they reduce exposure to auto traffic around the perimeter. Crossings are mandatory at 17th, 14th, 7th, 4th, and 1st Streets—all are

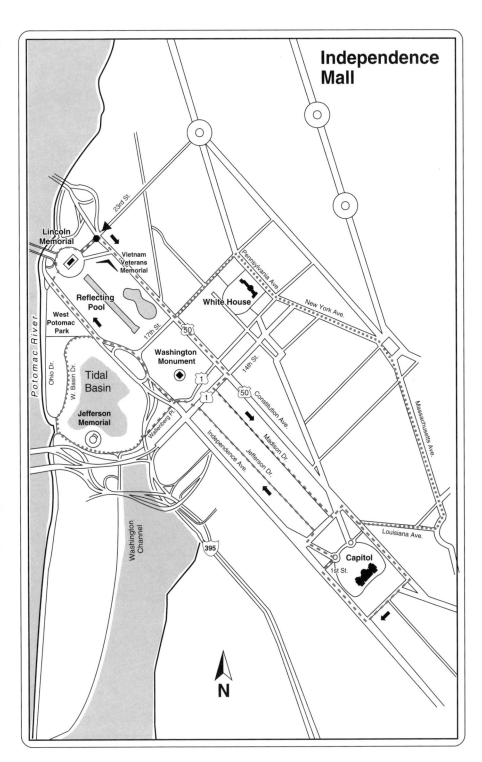

Independence Mall

Lincoln Memorial

Vietnam Veterans Memorial

Reflecting Pool

West Potomac Park

23rd St.

Potomac River

Ohio Dr.

W. Basin Dr.

Tidal Basin

Jefferson Memorial

Washington Monument

17th St.

Pennsylvania Ave.

White House

New York Ave.

14th St.

50

1

50

Constitution Ave.

Madison Dr.

Jefferson Dr.

Independence Ave.

Wallenberg Pl.

Washington Channel

395

Massachusetts Ave.

Louisiana Ave.

Capitol

1st St.

N

convenient, but caution is definitely required. Close calls are common here because cars occasionally run red lights and turn into pedestrian-filled crosswalks.

As you come to Capitol Hill, stay left on Constitution and follow the road up around the back of the Capitol. The hill is a bit steep, but the run through Capitol Plaza past the Supreme Court and the Library of Congress is worth the brief struggle. As for the rest of the scenery, the mile-long stretch west of the Capitol on either side provides a nonstop series of attractions, including the National Gallery of Art, the National Museum of Natural History, and the National Museum of American History on the north side, and the National Air and Space Museum and the Smithsonian to the south.

EXTENSIONS

If you'd like to postpone the climb up Capitol Hill, you can swing left on Louisiana Avenue just before the 1st Street crossing and take a brief 0.4-mile extension to Union Station, which is something of a tourist mecca with its scenic fountains. From there, you can also swing back to the White House for a closer view by taking a left onto Massachusetts Avenue and running 0.6 miles to Mount Vernon Square, then picking up New York Avenue on the opposite side of the square and continuing for 0.4 miles to 15th Street to pick up Pennsylvania Avenue.

On the opposite (south) side of the Mall, you can connect to the Tidal Basin loop by taking 15th Street south to Raoul Wallenberg Place at the U.S. Holocaust Memorial Museum. This connection is obvious as you run along this side of the Mall, but negotiating highway traffic can be a bit tricky. You can also run south from 17th Street to get to the Tidal Basin.

Finally, the end of the Mall loop puts you near the foot of the Arlington Memorial Bridge if you simply continue past the Lincoln Memorial, which allows you to pick up one of downtown D.C.'s primary bridge loops; descriptions follow.

ARLINGTON MEMORIAL BRIDGE– GEORGE MASON (14TH STREET) BRIDGE LOOP

3.3 MILES	TRAIL	SCENERY RATING	HILL RATING

ACCESS

You can reach both parking and a variety of starting points for this route from many different highways and major downtown arteries— check the map. The best parking options are the paid parking in Arlington National Cemetery, which puts you within a half mile of the Arlington Memorial Bridge, or the free lot in Lady Bird Johnson Park, which fills up quickly in good weather and can be accessed only while traveling west on the George Washington Memorial Parkway.

By subway, the best options are the Arlington Cemetery Metro station on the Virginia side or the Smithsonian Metro station in downtown D.C. From the Smithsonian stop, you can either run west through the Mall and then behind the Lincoln Memorial to get to the Arlington Memorial Bridge, or break off on either 17th Street or 15th Street to Raoul Wallenberg Place and run half of the Tidal Basin loop to get to the foot of the 14th Street Bridge.

COURSE

Like many river cities, Washington offers a series of point-to-point bridge routes. In this running category D.C. stands at the head of the urban class—you have your choice of no fewer than four bridges. The extra bonus is the array of terrain, from the relative isolation of the Chesapeake & Ohio Towpath on the D.C. side to the wild-and-woolly Potomac Heritage Trail on the Virginia side that connects the Key Bridge to the Chain Bridge.

This short bridge route is the hub of D.C. river running, offering excellent access to the downtown routes on the Washington side as well as the Mount Vernon Trail and Arlington National Cemetery on the Virginia side. Although there are many possible starting points, it's probably best to run it clockwise from west to east. This description begins from the Arlington Memorial Bridge, which is approximately 0.3 miles long.

Once you leave the bridge, head east and pick up either the footpath or the macadam bike path that runs along Ohio Drive. You'll see the Tidal Basin on your left; you can keep going to the footbridge that crosses over the basin, add a short loop on West Basin Drive, or divert completely to run the entire Tidal Basin loop. After crossing the small footbridge, pick up the bike path on the right side of the busy George Mason Bridge, known locally as the 14th Street Bridge.

As the trail breaks to the right off this bridge, you'll see the bike path near the river. At this point you'll be on the Mount Vernon Trail. You'll pass the LBJ Memorial as you run through Lady Bird Johnson Park, which is less than a park and slightly more than a rest stop on the Virginia side of the Potomac. Just before you return to the Arlington Memorial Bridge the bike trail breaks up a hill to the left toward the various highway crossings that are necessary to get back to the starting point.

EXTENSIONS AND OPTIONS

Besides connecting to the Tidal Basin loop, this route leads to many other downtown routes. After crossing the Arlington Memorial Bridge to the Maryland side, you can go straight to get to the Mall loop or go left to pick up the C&O Towpath, which also provides access to the Lower Rock Creek Park loop, the Key Bridge–Chain Bridge loop, and the Glover Archbold Park–Wesley Heights Park–Battery Kemble Park loop.

On the Virginia side, it's less than a half mile from the Arlington Memorial Bridge to the Arlington National Cemetery loop. You can also go north on the bike trail and pick up either the Potomac Heritage Trail or the street route for the Key Bridge–Chain Bridge loop. To the south, you'll find more than 15 miles of the Mount Vernon Trail to explore.

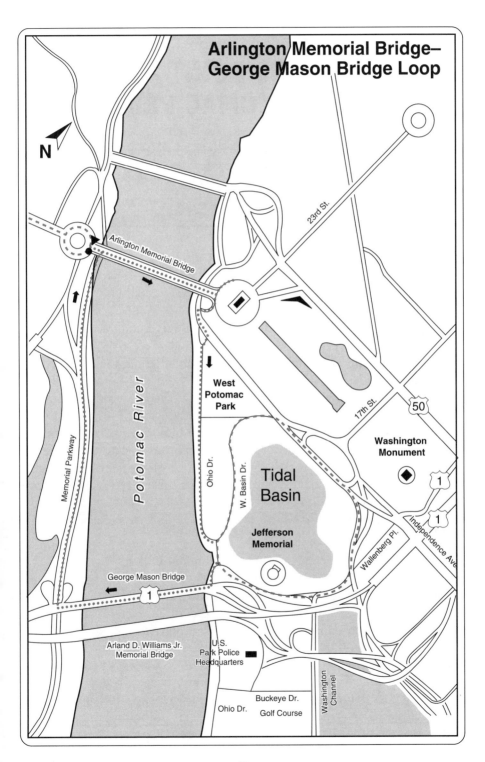

Arlington Memorial Bridge–
George Mason Bridge Loop

N

23rd St.

Arlington Memorial Bridge

Potomac River

Memorial Parkway

Ohio Dr.

W. Basin Dr.

West
Potomac
Park

Tidal
Basin

Jefferson
Memorial

17th St.

50

Washington
Monument

1

Wallenberg Pl.

Independence Ave.

1

George Mason Bridge

1

Arland D. Williams Jr.
Memorial Bridge

U.S.
Park Police
Headquarters

Washington
Channel

Buckeye Dr.

Ohio Dr.

Golf Course

HAINS POINT–
EAST POTOMAC PARK

3.5 MILES	ROAD	SCENERY RATING				
	👫 💧 ☎	HILL RATING				

ACCESS

Park at the National Park Service Headquarters, which you can reach by following the exit for East Potomac Park on Route 395. From the downtown area, the best driving bet is to follow Ohio Drive along the river until you enter the park and come to Buckeye Drive, where you can take a left and enter the park headquarters, which will also be on your left.

The best mass-transit option is again the Smithsonian Metro station, which requires a bit of a run to get to the park. Head west on Independence Avenue (toward the Lincoln Memorial end of the Mall), then take a left onto 15th Street, which becomes Raoul Wallenberg Place and leads to the Tidal Basin. Continue along the southeastern half of the Tidal Basin to the Potomac, then pick up Ohio Drive at the foot of the 14th Street Bridge.

COURSE

Because this loop around Hains Point takes you to the end of a peninsula, it provides a sense of escape within the confines of the downtown area. The run starts with a swing along the Potomac and some nice views of the Virginia side, and it closes with a view of Washington Channel Park and Fort McNair across the water.

The character of the run changes several times along the way. Initially it feels like a park run, especially if you're lucky enough to catch the spring contrast between the cherry blossoms and the greenery of the East Potomac Golf Course on your left. The south end of the park gets a bit scruffier as you approach Hains Point, making this run a questionable choice in twilight and a bad bet after dark. At the tip of

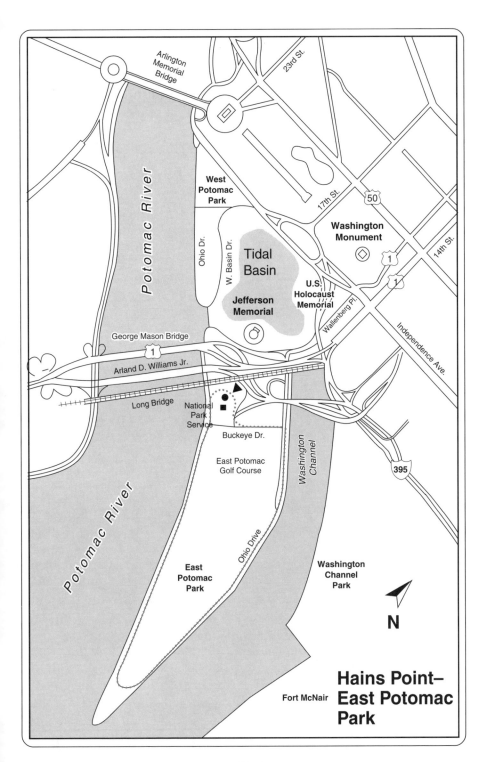

Hains Point–
East Potomac
Park

the Point is *The Awakening*—a giant bronze man whose feet, hands and head break through the ground and reach toward the sky.

Similarly, if you're getting to this route by either the 14th Street Bridge or the Tidal Basin loop, you'll want to be cautious around the underpass beneath the bridge, which is well lit but leaves you somewhat vulnerable for a brief 0.1-mile stretch.

NATIONAL ARBORETUM

2.6-4 MILES	ROAD	SCENERY RATING	
		HILL RATING	

ACCESS

While it is theoretically possible to run to this route from the Rhode Island Metro station, the urban blight of the surrounding area makes this choice inadvisable. Driving to the Arboretum is a bit tricky but much safer, and there are several parking areas within the grounds. The first choice is the main Visitors Center, which you can reach from the New York Avenue entrance.

If you're coming from downtown, go past the Capitol to Maryland Avenue, which angles northeast toward the park and runs into Bladensburg Avenue, which then intersects with New York Avenue. From the north, take exit 19 off the Beltway to Route 50, which heads southwest and turns into New York Avenue shortly after crossing Route 95. Follow the signs from the entrance to the Visitors Center, staying to the right after you enter the grounds. Parking is usually plentiful during the off-season, but the height of azalea season in late April and early May can produce considerable traffic or a parking crush.

COURSE

Like many of the best arboretums and botanical gardens in major cities across the country, Washington's National Arboretum represents an inner-city escape, in this case a boon to runners in a run-down area where good routes are few and far between. This loop is a bit short for distance work, but it includes some challenging hills, especially at the beginning of the course. What's unusual about this particular arboretum is that you run mostly on regular macadam roads rather than footpaths or dirt trails, which can seem a bit strange given the relative absence of cars.

This route starts from the Visitors Center and traces the perimeter of the grounds. If you're facing out toward the grounds from the Visitors

Center, head straight along Meadow Road (marked, but a bit hard to figure out), which quickly turns into Azalea Road.

The climb up Azalea is steep in a subtle sort of way, after which the road winds and turns into Crabtree Road.

The middle of the park is rather wide open—you'll be able to see the striking Capitol Columns on your left, and shortly after that you'll make a right onto Hickey Hill Road, which takes you into the Asian exhibit along the eastern perimeter. Except for the brief period when the azaleas are in bloom, this is the best part of the run—a long downhill after you make a left onto Conifer Road that takes you through the arboretum's excellent collection of dwarf conifers.

Road names have a habit of changing quickly on this run, and Conifer Road soon becomes Spring House Road, although at this point it's simpler to disregard the road signs and instead use the signs that take you through the last hill-and-dale section to the Visitors Center. For the botanically challenged who are here for the hill training, the perimeter loop measures 2.6 miles. Those with a penchant for meandering can milk some extra distance by taking any of the numerous short trails to view the various exhibits. An equally pleasant option is to explore the several short roads that bisect that park, making it possible to construct a number of ad hoc loops.

QUICK-AND-DIRTY DIRECTIONS

Straight: On Meadow Road to Azalea Road, which turns into Crabtree
    Road
Right: From Crabtree to Hickey Hill Road
Left: From Hickey Hill to Conifer Road, which turns into Spring House
    Road
Right: Onto Hickey Lane; follow signs for the Visitors Center

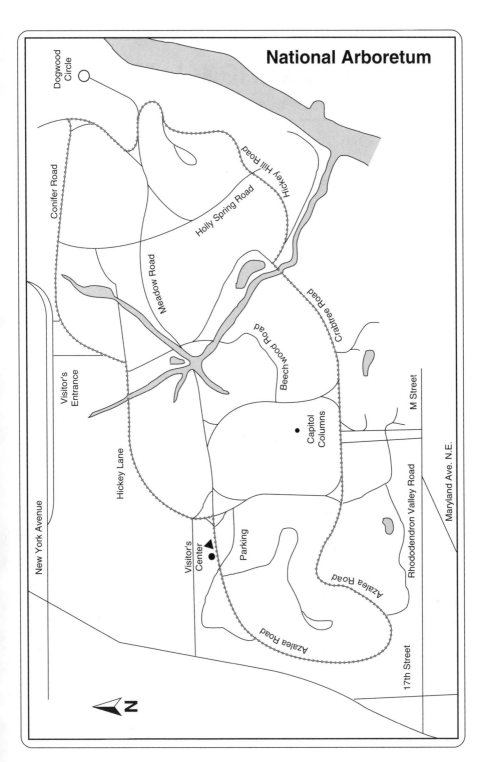

National Arboretum

Dogwood Circle

Conifer Road

Hickey Hill Road

Holly Spring Road

Meadow Road

Crabtree Road

Beech Wood Road

Visitor's Entrance

Hickey Lane

Capitol Columns

M Street

New York Avenue

Visitor's Center

Parking

Maryland Ave. N.E.

Rhododendron Valley Road

Azalea Road

Azalea Road

17th Street

N

ARLINGTON NATIONAL CEMETERY

| 4.9-5.3 MILES 👫 💧 ☎ | ROAD | SCENERY RATING | 🌳 🌳 🌳 🌳 🌳 |
| HILL RATING | ∿∿∿ |

ACCESS

The Arlington National Cemetery is located on Memorial Drive within a half mile of the Arlington Memorial Bridge on the Virginia side of the Potomac. You can reach it from a variety of roads, including Route 66, the George Washington Memorial Parkway, Constitution Avenue, Washington Boulevard, and Jefferson Davis Highway. There is paid parking within the grounds at a nominal rate of $1.50 per hour.

If you're accessing the run by mass transit, the Arlington Cemetery Metro station is just up the street from the entrance to the grounds on Memorial Drive.

COURSE

The loop around the perimeter of Arlington National Cemetery is one of Washington's prime running routes. Technically it's possible to run both inside the grounds and around the perimeter of the 612-acre cemetery. Both an inner and an outer loop are described here, but you'll want to check the official policy about running inside the cemetery, which can be quite confusing.

A phone call to the Arlington National Cemetery produced the official response that running was allowed as long as runners wore shirts, stayed on the roads, and respected ceremonies that were in progress on the grounds. However, it is not uncommon for cemetery employees to ask runners to walk while on the grounds, reducing the pace to a stolid run-walk. A more viable option may be to run early in the morning, when military personnel from the nearby Pentagon do their running, and when few ceremonies and funerals are in progress.

INNER LOOP

This 4.8-mile figure eight within the grounds starts just inside the Memorial Gate. Keep in mind that the length and exact path may change because roads may be closed for grounds work or ceremonies. But even with unexpected detours, it's fairly easy to trace a loop around the cemetery that will be just under 5 miles.

Take a right just after the Visitors Center onto Schley Drive, then take another right after 0.1 miles to Ord and Weitzel Drive, which climbs up and around the northern end of the cemetery until you reach Sherman Drive. If you take a right onto Sherman you'll enter a fairly congested area, so take a left and return to Schley Drive and head past the Memorial Gate again to complete the 1.8-mile loop on this side of the grounds.

After you pass through the gate, pick up Roosevelt Drive, which angles southwest through the center of the grounds. Go past McClellan Drive, where you'll see signs for the Kennedy grave site, and take a right onto Wilson Drive, then a left and a quick right onto Farragut Drive, which will take you to the western edge of the grounds. The left onto McPherson Drive leads to the southern section of the grounds. Then take a left on Clayton Drive, which eventually becomes Patton Drive and takes you to the eastern edge of the park.

As you pass the park service complex on your right, look for Patton Circle, then take a left onto Marshall Drive; this corner of the park houses the temporary facilities. Take a left onto York Drive, then a right onto either Halsey Drive or Eisenhower Drive to return to the front gate and the Visitors Center. Keep in mind, however, that Halsey Drive, while fairly isolated, is often used as a funeral route along the way to a series of administrative buildings that are tucked into the space between the parking lots and the Visitors Center.

OUTER LOOP

The 5.3-mile outer loop is a bit longer and requires some highway crossings, but there is a certain peace of mind in the certainty of an uninterrupted run.

As you approach the cemetery on Memorial Drive from the Arlington Memorial Bridge, take the first right turn after the Arlington Cemetery Metro entrance onto Route 110, the Jefferson Davis Highway. Follow the bike path that runs parallel to the highway as the road breaks to the left. At this point you'll have the option of taking a quick right onto the short path that leads to the Marine Memorial, which is worth the brief jog.

When you return to the bike path you'll pass through the gates of Fort Myer, where bicyclists are normally required to show identification. Continue up the hill on Marshall Drive and take the left branch of the fork onto McNair Road. Bear left at the parking lot as you come to the chapel and run parallel with the cemetery on either the dirt road next to the grounds or the roads that encircle them. As you head around the cemetery you'll come to the gate for Marine Corps Headquarters, where you'll enter and follow the road to the right past a guard post.

After you pass the guard post, take a left onto Southgate Road, then pick up the bike path at the first traffic light and follow it toward the Pentagon and then the Memorial Bridge. Follow the path underneath Route 27 (Washington Boulevard) to the Potomac side of the road, where you can enjoy the view along the river until the road intersects with Memorial Drive at the circle. Take a left at the circle and return to the Metro entrance.

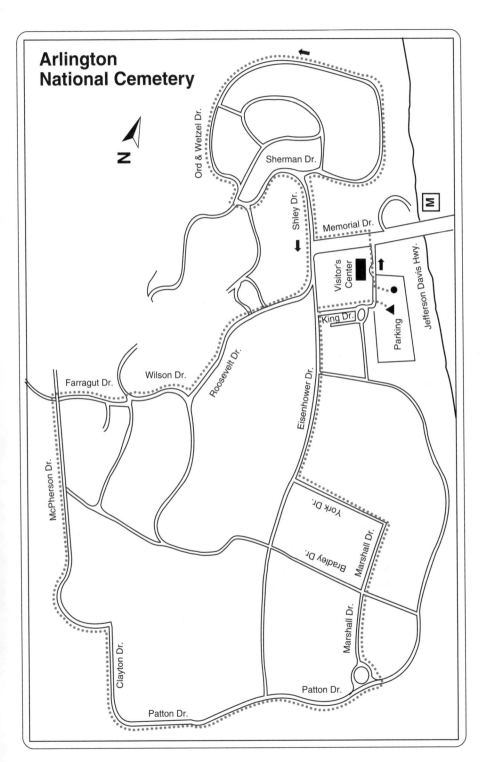

Arlington National Cemetery

N

Ord & Wetzel Dr.

Sherman Dr.

Shley Dr.

Memorial Dr.

M

Visitor's Center

Jefferson Davis Hwy.

King Dr.

Parking

Farragut Dr.

Wilson Dr.

Roosevelt Dr.

Eisenhower Dr.

McPherson Dr.

York Dr.

Bradley Dr.

Marshall Dr.

Marshall Dr.

Clayton Dr.

Patton Dr.

Patton Dr.

ROOSEVELT ISLAND

1.6 MILES	TRAIL	SCENERY RATING	
	🚻 💧 ☎	HILL RATING	

ACCESS

The exit for the Roosevelt Island parking lot can be reached going west from the George Washington Memorial Parkway. The best mass-transit option on the Virginia side is the Arlington Cemetery Metro station, which requires a 1-mile run along Memorial Drive and then west on the Mount Vernon Trail to get to the island. From the Maryland side, the Foggy Bottom stop is the closest choice—head south on 23rd Street to the Mall, run behind the Lincoln Memorial and across the Arlington Memorial Bridge, then west on the Mount Vernon Trail to get to the island.

COURSE

Like the Tidal Basin loop on the Maryland side, the loop around Roosevelt Island is too short to run as a stand-alone route, but it does connect easily to many other downtown options, most notably the Arlington Memorial Bridge–Key Bridge loop.

The island itself is an 88-acre wilderness preserve that was designed as a tribute to Theodore Roosevelt's devotion to conservation. After you cross the wooden footbridge from the parking lot to the island, there's an outer loop that runs around the perimeter of the island, along with a trail that leads to the center and a larger-than-life statue of the "Rough Rider." For the most part the trails are wide and spacious, although they become somewhat narrow on the west side of the island and contain exposed tree roots in many areas along the way.

Finally, there are several short, deceptive dead-end trails that can become tedious; the best way to avoid them is to run the island counterclockwise.

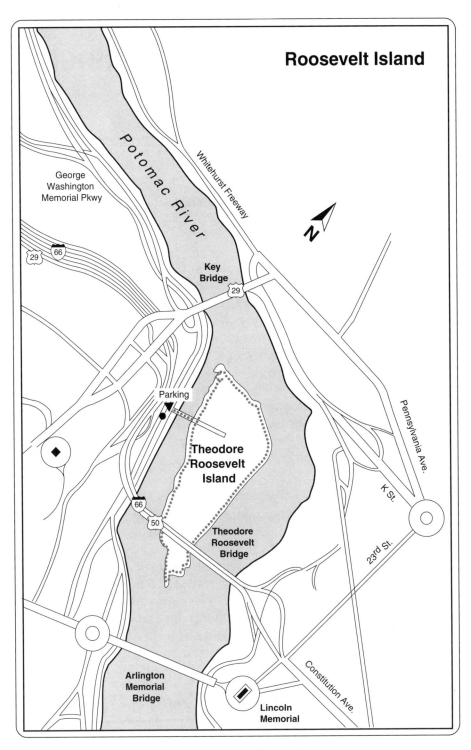

Roosevelt Island

George Washington Memorial Pkwy

Potomac River

Whitehurst Freeway

N

29

66

Key Bridge

29

Parking

Theodore Roosevelt Island

66

50

Theodore Roosevelt Bridge

Pennsylvania Ave.

K St.

23rd St.

Constitution Ave.

Arlington Memorial Bridge

Lincoln Memorial

ARLINGTON MEMORIAL BRIDGE–
KEY BRIDGE LOOP

2.8 MILES	TRAIL	SCENERY RATING					
		HILL RATING					

ACCESS

By car, the easiest access to this route is from the Roosevelt Island parking lot, which you can reach by going *west* on the George Washington Memorial Parkway to the Roosevelt Island exit. You can also spring for paid parking in the Arlington National Cemetery ($1.50 per hour), park in Georgetown beyond the Key Bridge (two-hour metered parking and some free two-hour parking), or park off Constitution on one of the side streets (17th Street to 23rd Street, two-hour metered parking).

The mass-transit options include the Arlington National Cemetery stop just down the street from the Arlington Memorial Bridge, or the Foggy Bottom station, from which you can run south on 23rd Street to get to the Mall loop, then behind the Lincoln Memorial to pick up the Arlington Memorial Bridge.

COURSE

The shortest of the three downtown bridge loops, this route offers just enough distance to be viable as a stand-alone route, but its primary value is its potential as a connector to the western downtown routes.

The most obvious connection here is for Roosevelt Island (see previous route), but this is also an excellent way to get to lower Rock Creek Park, the Glover Archbold Park–Wesley Heights Park–Battery Kemble Park loop, or any of the routes involving the C&O Towpath on the Maryland side. On the Virginia side, you can get to Arlington National Cemetery easily or add to the bridge count by heading over to the 14th Street Bridge. If you want distance, you can go all the way out to the Chain Bridge and back.

If you're starting from Roosevelt Island, run clockwise by heading west to the Key Bridge. Right after you leave the parking lot you'll have

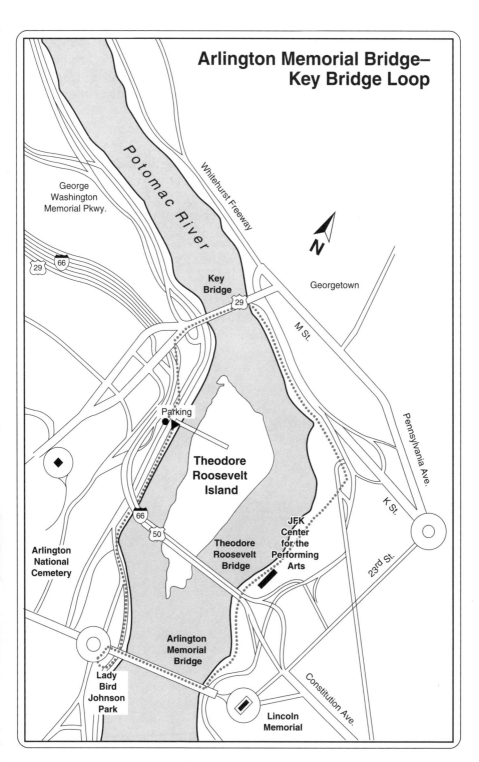

Arlington Memorial Bridge–
Key Bridge Loop

Potomac River

George
Washington
Memorial Pkwy.

Whitehurst Freeway

29 66

Key
Bridge

29

Georgetown

M St.

Parking

Theodore
Roosevelt
Island

Pennsylvania Ave.

K St.

66

50

JFK
Center
for the
Performing
Arts

Arlington
National
Cemetery

Theodore
Roosevelt
Bridge

23rd St.

Arlington
Memorial
Bridge

Lady
Bird
Johnson
Park

Constitution Ave.

Lincoln
Memorial

a choice of following the bike path (which leads to the end of the Mount Vernon Trail) across the highway to get to the Key Bridge, or you can stay along the water and pick up the blue-blazed Potomac Heritage Trail if you're up for a rough-and-tumble journey out to the Chain Bridge.

Once you cross the Key Bridge, stay to the right and you'll come to a tiny park on the corner that leads down to the C&O Towpath. From there you can either break off the towpath to the Rock Creek Park loop or follow the towpath until it ends just short of the Arlington Memorial Bridge and the Mall loop. A ramp at the end of the Arlington Memorial Bridge takes you back down to the water and onto the Mount Vernon Trail, where you can run to the finish at the Roosevelt Island parking lot.

ROCK CREEK PARK– NATIONAL ZOO (LOWER LOOP)

6.4 MILES	TRAIL 👫 💧 📞	SCENERY RATING	🌳 🌳 🌳 🌳
		HILL RATING	⛰️

ACCESS

Metered and garage parking are available near the start of this run along Virginia Avenue and 18th Street through 25th Street, and from F through M streets, although you may have to do some hunting for a quiet side street.

The best mass-transit option is the Foggy Bottom station; head south on 23rd Street and then northwest on Virginia Avenue to the beginning of Rock Creek Parkway.

COURSE

In a city laced with urban greenspace, Rock Creek Park is D.C.'s prime getaway course. This loop takes you through the lower stretch of the park, which you can extend through the National Zoological Park. One of Washington's most popular downtown loops, this route can also be extended into some top-notch trail running as a one-way mass-transit run from Silver Spring to the downtown section of Rock Creek (see "Parks and Paths: Suburbs and Exurbs").

The downtown loop begins at the intersection of Virginia Avenue and Rock Creek Parkway. Head north on the bike path that runs to the left alongside Rock Creek Parkway. An alternate route is the footpath on the other side of the creek. Rock Creek Parkway is a busy highway, giving the first 2 miles an urban character.

Just beyond the 2-mile mark you'll come to a brief tunnel, where you'll have a couple choices. You can continue through the tunnel and run the route as an out-and-back. Another option is to pick up the Polar Bear path halfway through the loop around the tunnel (it's marked by blue pawprints on the road) and explore the zoo grounds briefly.

The official turnaround point for the prescribed 6.4-mile out-and-back is Park Road, which is just beyond where the Rock Creek Park trail bends to the left along Beach Drive.

EXTENSIONS AND OPTIONS

This part of Rock Creek Park connects with many other routes. If you take the tunnel under Canal Road from the starting point, you'll be on the C&O Towpath, where you can go west to the Key Bridge, the Glover Archbold Park–Wesley Heights Park–Battery Kemble Park loop (description follows), or the Capital Crescent Trail (see chapter 2) and the Chain Bridge beyond.

Head southeast and you'll quickly come to the beginning of the Mall loop and the Arlington Memorial Bridge, from which you can access a host of downtown runs described earlier in this section.

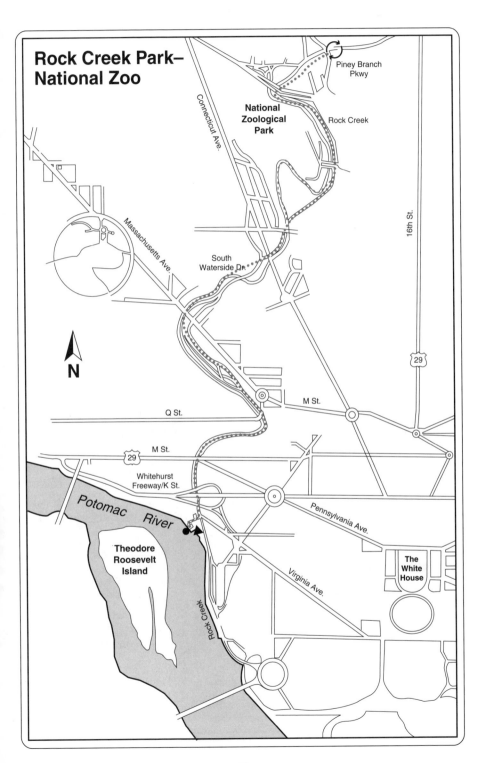

Rock Creek Park–
National Zoo

National Zoological Park

Rock Creek

Piney Branch Pkwy

Connecticut Ave.

16th St.

Massachusetts Ave.

South Waterside Dr.

N

29

M St.

Q St.

29 M St.

Whitehurst Freeway/K St.

Pennsylvania Ave.

Potomac River

Theodore Roosevelt Island

Rock Creek

Virginia Ave.

The White House

GLOVER ARCHBOLD PARK–
WESLEY HEIGHTS PARK–
BATTERY KEMBLE PARK LOOP

3-7.5 MILES	ROAD/TRAIL	SCENERY RATING	🌳🌳🌳🌳
	💧 ☎	HILL RATING	⛰⛰⛰

ACCESS

The best place to park for this run is in Georgetown near the Key Bridge. Take a right off the bridge heading toward D.C. and then a quick left to find metered parking on M Street or, if you're low on quarters, two-hour free on-street parking along N to P Streets.

By mass transit, use the Foggy Bottom Metro station—pick up Washington Circle and head west on Pennsylvania Avenue, which runs into M Street as you head out toward the Key Bridge. From the Key Bridge you can run along the C&O Towpath to the first underpass, which takes you beneath Canal Road. Make a left after the underpass and pick up the trail on the right just beyond a small grassy field. Another alternative to the towpath is Canal Road itself, which has plenty of safe sidewalk space and offers more direct access to the trailhead.

COURSE

This H-shaped route linking three relatively small parks is one of the most unusual and appealing in the downtown area, but because it's a bit out of the way it often becomes lost in the urban shuffle. Besides offering some fine park scenery, the trails are well marked and easy to follow, with mileage postings along the way.

The route starts on the Maryland side of the Potomac halfway between the Key Bridge and the Georgetown Reservoir. The trailhead is off Canal Road, on the north side of the road just beyond a grassy field before Canal meets Foxhall Road.

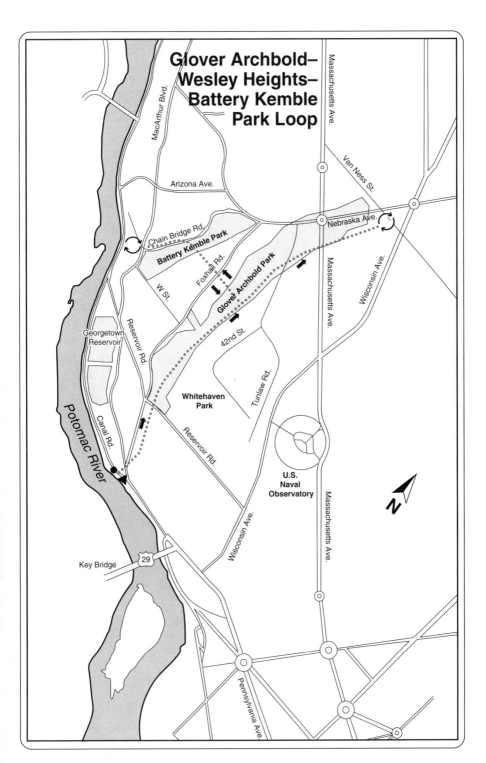

Glover Archbold–
Wesley Heights–
Battery Kemble
Park Loop

MacArthur Blvd.

Massachusetts Ave.

Arizona Ave.

Van Ness St.

Chain Bridge Rd.

Nebraska Ave.

Battery Kemble Park

Foxhall Rd.

Glover Archbold Park

W St.

Massachusetts Ave.

Wisconsin Ave.

Reservoir Rd.

Georgetown
Reservoir

42nd St.

Tunlaw Rd.

Whitehaven
Park

Canal Rd.

Reservoir Rd.

Potomac River

U.S.
Naval
Observatory

Massachusetts Ave.

N

Wisconsin Ave.

Key Bridge

29

Pennsylvania Ave.

Glover Archbold Park is level and pleasant, with mileage markers that dictate both the route and some possible turnoffs. If you run all the way to Van Ness Street as an out-and-back, the total distance is 6.4 miles; you can also turn around at Massachusetts Avenue, which is 2 miles out.

If you're park hopping, the first option choice comes at the 1.5-mile mark. Take a right and you can pick up the Whitehaven Trail to Rock Creek Park; a left takes you through narrow Wesley Heights Park for 0.8 miles until you come to Battery Kemble Park, which forms the other leg of the H. It's easy to become turned around in Battery Kemble; make sure you *cross* Foxhall Road in the middle of this section at the posted mileage marker.

Battery Kemble is the last leg, a short, narrow 1.3-mile park that extends from MacArthur Boulevard to Nebraska Avenue. It's the busiest and least green of the three parks, particularly as you head north up a fairly steep hill that leads to Nebraska Avenue. You can also continue northwest on MacArthur Boulevard and then take a left onto Arizona Avenue to get down to the C&O Towpath. Be aware that the road shoulders narrow steadily along the way and you will have to negotiate some tricky highway crossings as you head downhill on Arizona.

KEY BRIDGE–CHAIN BRIDGE LOOP

7.5 MILES	TRAIL	SCENERY RATING	
	🚻 💧 📞	HILL RATING	

ACCESS

Several parking options are available for this run. The Roosevelt Island parking lot off the George Washington Memorial Parkway (going west) puts you at the foot of the Potomac Heritage Trail. On the Maryland side, the streets around Georgetown (M to P) near the foot of the Key Bridge are the best bet for metered or free on-street parking.

The best mass-transit option is the Rosslyn Metro station on the Virginia side, from which you emerge at the corner of 19th Street and Moore Street. Run west on Moore and take a left to the beginning of the Custis Trail as you approach the Key Bridge to access the street version of this run, or take a right and follow the bike trail down to the Roosevelt Island parking lot, where you can pick up the Potomac Heritage Trail.

On the Maryland side, the Foggy Bottom Metro station is the best choice, but you'll have to run northwest on Virginia Avenue and pick up the C&O Towpath near the beginning of Rock Creek Park.

COURSE

The loop from the Key Bridge to the Chain Bridge is the longest and wildest of Washington's bridge loops, especially if you choose the rugged Potomac Heritage Trail to get to the Chain Bridge on the Virginia side (alternate street directions are also provided). The Maryland side is more sedate, covering the initial sections of the C&O Towpath.

This description assumes a starting point from the Potomac Heritage Trail, which you can access from the Roosevelt Island parking lot. There you'll see mileage figures for the blue-blazed trail at the foot of the bridge on the Mount Vernon Trail just before it breaks back across the George Washington Parkway. This starting point adds an extra tenth of a mile or two, but it's safer than trying to execute the highway crossings from the Key Bridge itself down to the trail, which runs right along the water.

The Potomac Heritage Trail remains runnable for the first 3 miles to the Chain Bridge, although there are a few rocky sections and some tricky small hills when the trail breaks back from the Potomac. (Keep in mind that this trail is dangerous in ice and snow.) The last quarter to half mile, however, is a virtual rock scramble that will destroy any hopes of a PR. The blue blazes are relatively easy to pick up as you go from rock to rock, and the trail ends with a short, sharp hill down the belly of an underpass to the foot of the Key Bridge.

STREET ROUTE (ALTERNATE TO POTOMAC HERITAGE TRAIL)

The street route from the Key Bridge to Chain Bridge on the Virginia side adds extra mileage, but it's considerably safer and easier than the Potomac Heritage Trail, and a better option for those who don't prefer trail running. From the Key Bridge, pick up the Custis Trail, a macadam bike path that runs parallel to I-66. At the Lee Highway, double back on the trail and pick up Lorcom Lane, then take a right onto Nellie Custis Drive, which takes you to Military Road. Follow Military Road until it ends at Williamsburg Boulevard (Route 120), then take a right to the Chain Bridge.

After you cross the Chain Bridge, the Maryland side of the Potomac is a breeze by comparison. From the bridge follow a winding path down to the C&O Towpath, which was built in the early 1800s and extends 184 miles from Georgetown in Washington, D.C., to Cumberland, Maryland. The towpath is maintained for running, bicycling, and hiking by the National Park Service. Because it is susceptible to flood damage, conditions are subject to change. The 3.2 miles of towpath offer a choice of a bike path or the oft-muddy canal footpath, and within a half mile of the Chain Bridge you'll also pass the trestle bridge that connects to the Capital Crescent Trail.

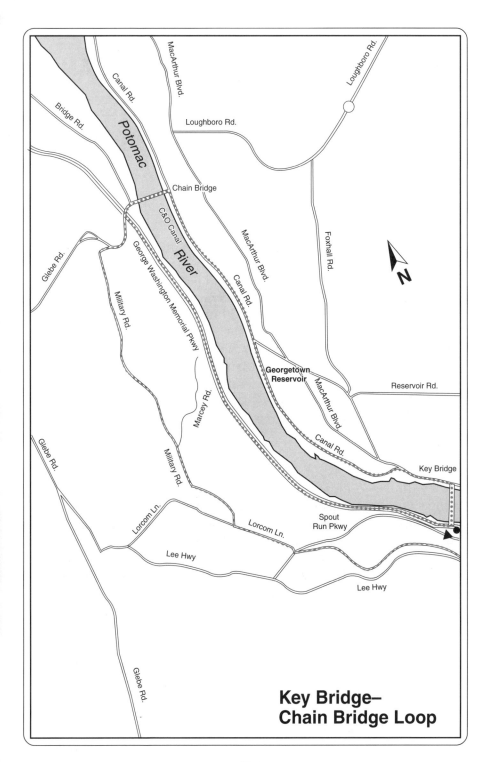

**Key Bridge–
Chain Bridge Loop**

UPPER MOUNT VERNON TRAIL

5 MILES	TRAIL	SCENERY RATING	
	👫 💧 ☎	HILL RATING	

ACCESS

Parking at either end of this route is easy and convenient from the George Washington Memorial Parkway. If you're starting from Roosevelt Island, use the lot across from the island; similarly, there's an exit for Gravelly Point off the parkway on the northbound side.

Mass transit for this route is feasible, but tricky. You can start from the Arlington Cemetery and pick up the bike path off Memorial Drive before the Memorial Bridge—this will cut some distance from the route. From the south, the closest Metro station is the National Airport, which means dealing with considerable airport traffic. You could also use the Pentagon station or the Pentagon City stop, although you really have to be familiar with the area to get down to the river.

COURSE

The northern section of the Mount Vernon Trail offers some Potomac views similar to those of other runs in this section, but this stretch allows you to catch some spectacular "under-the-wing" views from National Airport. Even though it's an out-and-back route, this part of the trail is fairly flexible, allowing you to go farther south on the Mount Vernon Trail or pick up the Arlington National Cemetery run, the loop around Theodore Roosevelt Island, or one of the many bridge loops.

The course covers miles 15 to 17 of the Mount Vernon Trail, which begins at mile 0 downriver at Mount Vernon. The run along Gravelly Point adds a half mile in either direction, bringing the final tally to around 5 miles. It offers perhaps the most extended and unimpeded views of downtown D.C. of any route in this section.

To extend the run or make additional connections to the south, continue along the Mount Vernon Trail toward Daingerfield Island or Old Town Alexandria (see directions for the Central Mount Vernon Trail on page 65). To the north, the Roosevelt Island starting point puts you close to Arlington National Cemetery and a variety of bridge routes.

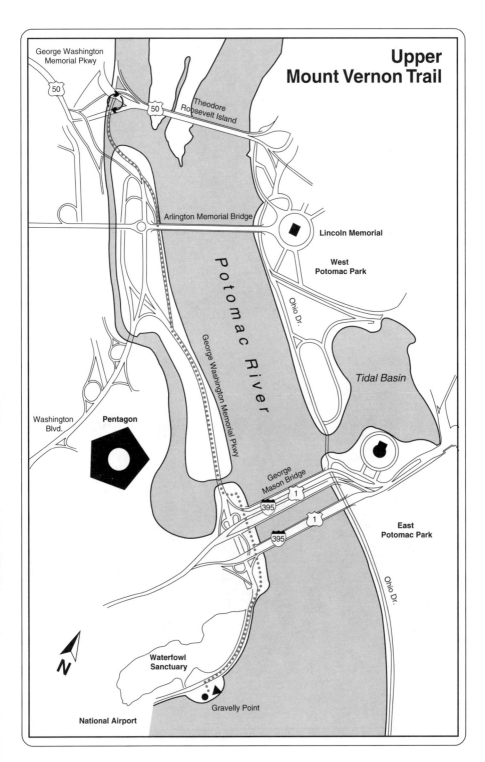

Upper Mount Vernon Trail

George Washington Memorial Pkwy

Theodore Roosevelt Island

Arlington Memorial Bridge

Lincoln Memorial

West Potomac Park

Ohio Dr.

Potomac River

George Washington Memorial Pkwy

Tidal Basin

Washington Blvd.

Pentagon

George Mason Bridge

East Potomac Park

Ohio Dr.

Waterfowl Sanctuary

Gravelly Point

National Airport

N

PATHS AND PARKS: SUBURBS AND EXURBS

1. Rock Creek Park (Silver Spring to Downtown)
2. Rock Creek Regional Park (Montgomery County)
3. Ken Gar Palisades Park to Lake Needwood Regional Park
4. Ken Gar Palisades Park to Meadowbrook Park
5. Four-Mile Run West—Washington & Old Dominion Trail–Custis Trail
6. Four-Mile Run East—Bluemont Park to Barcroft Park
7. Capital Crescent Trail, Northern Section (Bethesda to Massachusetts Avenue)
8. Capital Crescent Trail, Southern Section (Massachusetts Avenue to C&O Towpath)
9. Central Mount Vernon Trail (Daingerfield Island to Alexandria)
10. Southern Mount Vernon Trail (Mount Vernon to Fort Hunt Park)
11. Northeast Branch–Northwest Branch Trails (With Metro Connector)
12. Lake Artemesia
13. Sligo Creek Trail South–Long Branch Loop
14. Greenbelt Park
15. Wakefield Park, Lake Acotink
16. Patuxent Wildlife Refuge
17. Battlefield Park, Stone Bridge Trail

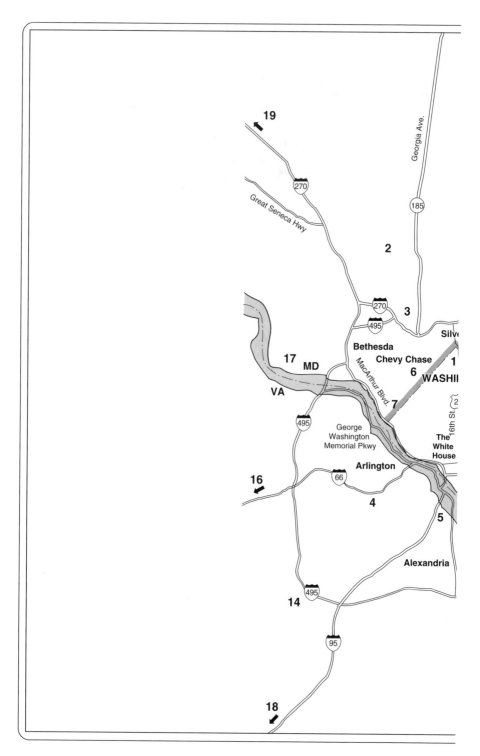

Paths and Parks:
Suburbs and Exurbs

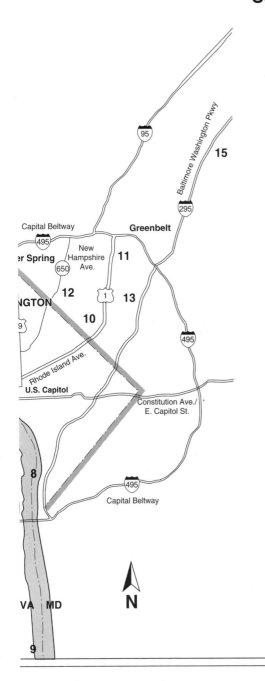

95

Baltimore Washington Pkwy

15

295

Capital Beltway

Greenbelt

495

er Spring

650

New Hampshire Ave.

11

12

NGTON

9

1

13

10

495

Rhode Island Ave.

U.S. Capitol

Constitution Ave./ E. Capitol St.

8

495

Capital Beltway

VA | **MD**

N

9

18. Chesapeake & Ohio (C&O) Canal Towpath, Great Falls Park
19. Prince William Forest
20. Seneca Creek State Park

INTRODUCTION

Although this section includes some runs that are relatively close to downtown D.C., the primary focus is on the outlying areas. The foundation for this section is Washington's excellent network of bike trails, which in many cases you can combine with the trails in the regional park system to put together routes that offer both road and trail running.

If there's a downside to this approach, it's that the bike paths create mostly out-and-back routes. Wherever possible, longer runs along a particular bike path have been broken up into 2- to 3-mile segments that you can combine for race or marathon training.

Although you can reach most of the runs in this section easily only by car, you can use the Metro on several routes to cover either the front or back end, allowing you to run the route as a one-way. While bus access is theoretically possible, the combination of changing buses and waiting in unseasonable conditions for the appropriate bus to arrive was deemed too impractical for all but the hardiest of runners.

As you consider these routes, keep in mind some of the possible long-run combinations. The Custis Trail, Four-Mile Run, and the Washington & Old Dominion (W & OD) Trail, for instance, all converge near the center of Arlington, and the downtown bridges can be augmented with either a jaunt along the Potomac River on the Mount Vernon Trail or a run up the Potomac using the Chesapeake & Ohio (C&O) Canal Towpath. With a little imagination, it's easy to develop an extensive network of "homegrown" runs using this section as a foundation.

ROCK CREEK PARK (SILVER SPRING TO DOWNTOWN)

10.3 MILES	TRAIL	SCENERY RATING	
	👫 💧 ☎	HILL RATING	

ACCESS

This run starts from the Silver Spring Metro Station, which is on the Red Line north of the downtown area. If you're driving and dropping a car at the beginning of the run, park near the Foggy Bottom station on the Blue Line, located on 23rd Street near Washington Circle next to George Mason University. Both metered parking and garage parking is available in the immediate area.

From there, take the Metro three stops from Foggy Bottom to Metro Center, then switch to the Red Line north and get off at the Silver Spring Station. The run starts with a left onto Colesville Road just outside the station.

COURSE

This long run takes you through the two lower sections of Rock Creek Park, each half of which has a distinct character. The first half presents a tough, hilly trail run on the Valley Trail that traces a path south through the park to the National Zoo. The second half, which leads to the Potomac, is more urban in character, and is also covered in the section on downtown Washington.

UPPER SECTION

As you emerge from the station, take a left onto Colesville and run for a quarter mile to the intersection of Colesville Road and 16th Street. Cross 16th Street and pick up North Portal Drive, a short suburban road that you'll run on for approximately a half mile until it ends at East Beach Drive. Take a left onto East Beach, then look immediately for Kalma Road and take a right onto Kalma and a quick left onto West Beach Drive, which is actually in Rock Creek Park.

Within a tenth of a mile you'll see Parkside Drive on your right, just before Parkside. Look for the trail entrance on your left in the park. At this point you'll be heading south with the creek on your right, running on an unmarked bridle path sans blazes. After about a mile you'll see signs for the Valley Trail, a foot trail that joins the bridle trail until you reach the Riley Spring Bridge, where the bridle path crosses the water. Stay on the Valley Trail, which is marked by blue blazes—the creek will be on your right.

You'll remain on the Valley Trail for approximately the next 4 miles until you reach Park Road just north of the zoo, where the run becomes much more urban. The Valley Trail is demanding and hilly, and generally well marked and easy to follow except for a couple short stretches. One such place is the Military Road crossing, where the trail goes uphill and back away from the road briefly to get around a busy section of highway.

When you cross the road you'll see the Park Police Substation. Keep the station on your left and look for the blue marker on the left after you pass it, but whatever you do don't take the left before the station onto Morrow Drive. The two meanest hills on the route occur near the end (of course), just before you descend onto Park Road, where you'll take a left and follow the macadam path.

LOWER SECTION

Once you reach Park Road, you'll be running along Rock Creek Parkway as well as the creek itself, with a choice of a sidewalk next to the highway or the bike path on the other (right) side of the creek. Just after you pass the entrance for the National Zoo you'll come to a tunnel where you can either pass through or take the loop that goes around and into the zoo (the zoo extension is described in the downtown section).

The unofficial end of the run is the Thompson Boat House, which is off to the right at the traffic light just short of the Potomac. Take a left onto Virginia Avenue and follow it past the Watergate Hotel to 23rd Street, which takes you back to the Foggy Bottom Metro station.

ALTERNATE UPPER LOOPS

The upper sections of Rock Creek Park contain an extensive trail network. By using the excellent trail map published by the Park Service, you can put together a number of alternate routes.

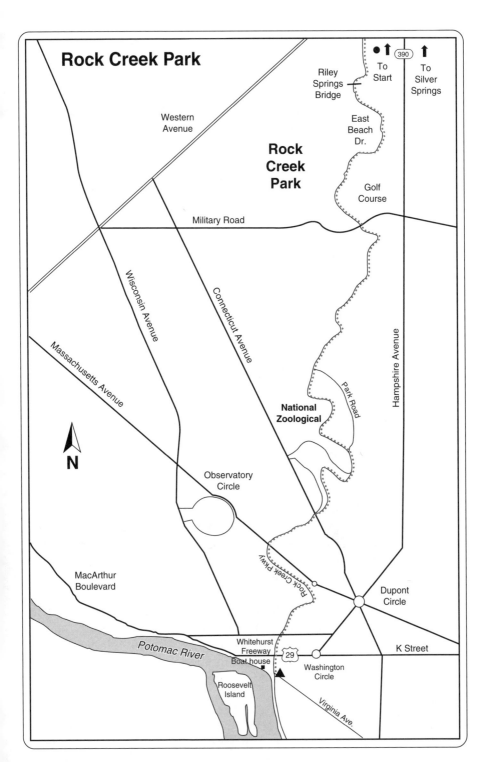

Rock Creek Park

Riley Springs Bridge

To Start

To Silver Springs

Western Avenue

Rock Creek Park

East Beach Dr.

Golf Course

Military Road

Wisconsin Avenue

Connecticut Avenue

Hampshire Avenue

Massachusetts Avenue

Park Road

National Zoological

N

Observatory Circle

MacArthur Boulevard

Rock Creek Pkwy

Dupont Circle

Potomac River

Whitehurst Freeway

Boat house

K Street

Washington Circle

Roosevelt Island

Virginia Ave.

KEN GAR PALISADES PARK TO LAKE NEEDWOOD REGIONAL PARK

2-14.5 MILES	TRAIL	SCENERY RATING	
	👫 💧 ☎	HILL RATING	

To get to some of the best routes in the 23 miles of Rock Creek Park running terrain, you'll have to take a quick trip north to Montgomery County. The upper section of the park offers wooded beauty and seclusion far different from the routes south of the Beltway. Rock Creek has also seen its share of political celebrities, from Teddy Roosevelt on horseback to our most recent jogging presidents.

The Montgomery County section of the park has a 13-mile contiguous macadam bike and running path that follows the creek from Lake Needwood to Meadowbrook Stables, which is one mile north of the D.C. line. The mileposts begin at this line and continue north to the mile-14 marker at the lake, using the same precise measurement standards that are used to certify race courses.

The path has numerous side trails, but the main trail is usually obvious and well marked, thanks in part to considerable assistance from the Montgomery County Road Runners Club, which has worked with the Park Service to place mile markers, bulletin boards, and fountains in the park.

ACCESS

Take the Rockville Pike north (Route 355) from the Beltway (I-495). Turn right on Strathmore Road just north of the Grosvenor Metro station, then take a left at the first light onto Beach Drive. Park for free at Ken Gar Palisades Park in the center of the Montgomery County section of Rock Creek Park, which is on the right just after the railroad overpass.

COURSE

This out-and-back path runs north through Rock Creek Park to Lake Needwood Regional Park, with a distance range from 2 to 14.5 miles,

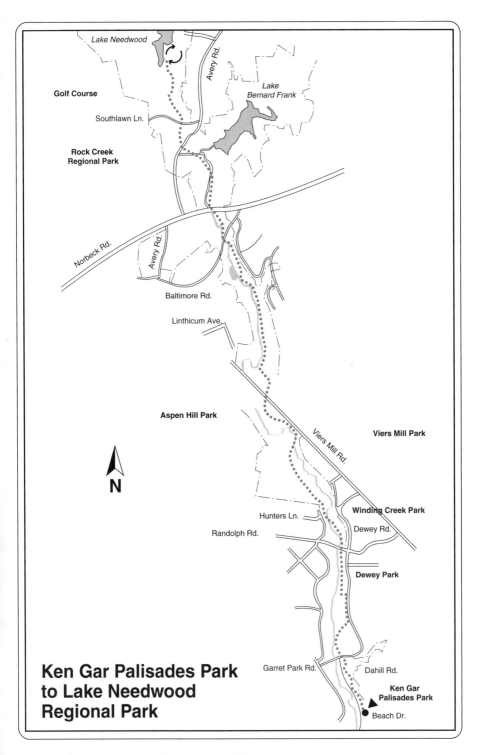

Lake Needwood

Avery Rd.

Golf Course

Lake
Bernard Frank

Southlawn Ln.

Rock Creek
Regional Park

Norbeck Rd.

Avery Rd.

Baltimore Rd.

Linthicum Ave.

Aspen Hill Park

Viers Mill Rd.

Viers Mill Park

N

Winding Creek Park

Hunters Ln.

Dewey Rd.

Randolph Rd.

Dewey Park

Ken Gar Palisades Park
to Lake Needwood
Regional Park

Garret Park Rd.

Dahill Rd.

Ken Gar
Palisades Park

Beach Dr.

depending on the selected turnaround point. It has a slightly more isolated feel than the southern section and is also a bit hillier, with a number of jagged rock outcrops along the way.

From the Ken Gar parking lot, head north from the mile-7 marker just beyond the basketball court. From here the path runs parallel with Beach Drive, winding through woods with homes to the right and Beach Drive to left. You'll cross two small footbridges over side streams along the way. After you cross Garret Park Road you'll enter Viers Mill Park and pass a playground and a field, then go up a short but steep hill to Dewey Park at mile 8.

Pass the tennis courts in the park and take the path to the left, then make an immediate right into the woods and cross the footbridge. After passing a small open area, you'll cross Randolph Road at the light; the path continues to the left and follows the edge of a large field to a water fountain. Turn left at the fountain and cross the footbridge over Rock Creek, then take an immediate right and continue uphill into the woods to mile 9.

The next mile covers a hilly stretch through dense woods before the path intersects with a service road, crosses Rock Creek on the service road bridge, and then bears left just before the service road intersects with Viers Mill Road. The next crossing is at Parklawn Memorial Park Road, after which you'll run along the west side of a large field before crossing Viers Mill Road at the next light.

Follow the bike-route signs and make an immediate left onto Adrian Street after you cross Viers Mill Road. Then turn left into the Aspen Hill Park parking lot and pick up the path again at the water fountain. The path levels out and continues through the woods with Rock Creek on the left until you reach the mile-11 marker.

From this point the trail runs parallel to the creek all the way to Lake Needwood, with a slight hill just before mile 12 (at this point you've run 5 miles). Shortly thereafter you'll cross Baltimore Road, which you should approach with caution, as visibility is limited, the traffic is fast moving, and there's no light.

After a wooded section with small hills you'll pass under a major road overpass, then cross Rock Creek twice just before mile 13. The next two road crossings are at Avery Road and Southlawn Lane. Approach each cautiously. A short, steep 0.2-mile hill takes you away from the creek just before mile 14, after which you'll run for 0.25 miles on the path through a parking lot to Lake Needwood Regional Park and the Visitors Center (closed in winter).

KEN GAR PALISADES PARK TO MEADOWBROOK PARK

2-12 MILES	TRAIL	SCENERY RATING	
	🚻 💧 📞	HILL RATING	

Those who want to extend their runs south have two options. First is the previously described trail run from the Silver Spring Metro station to the Potomac. Second, key sections of the road in this part of Rock Creek Park are closed to vehicles on weekends, making it possible to run from Meadowbrook Stables into the District of Columbia. Once you're in the district, you can pick up the bike path at Pierce Mill north of the National Zoo and hook up with the Rock Creek Park–National Zoo route, which is also outlined in the section on downtown running.

ACCESS

Take the Rockville Pike north (Route 355) from the Beltway (I-495). Turn right on Strathmore just north of the Grosvenor Metro station, then take a left at the first light onto Beach Drive. Park for free at Ken Gar Palisades Park in the center of the Montgomery County section of Rock Creek Park, which is on the right just after the railroad overpass.

COURSE

This out-and-back run with a distance range of 2 to 12 miles takes you south through Rock Creek Park to Meadowbrook Riding Stables. It runs through a densely populated suburban residential area, past several street crossings without lights where caution is essential. But the route also includes lengthy stretches through relatively deep woods over gently rolling hills with some pleasant flat stretches.

From the Ken Gar parking lot, start at mile 7 just beyond the basketball court and run south. Again, the path runs parallel to Beach Drive, then crosses Knowles Avenue at a traffic light after the railroad overpass. From there you run through a short stretch of rolling hills before the trail bears left into the woods, with Rock Creek on the right until you come to mile 6.

At this point the path breaks away from Rock Creek for about a half mile as you head through a hilly wooded section, after which it picks up the creek again after crossing Beach Drive shortly before the mile-5 marker at a footbridge. The path then winds next to Rock Creek with Beach Drive on the left and the creek on the right, crossing Cedar Lane at a stoplight and continuing along the creek to mile 4.

After that you'll go through a tunnel under Connecticut Avenue, running through a low stretch that can become muddy and slippery after heavy rain. A short side trail to the left just before mile 4 leads to a traffic-light crossing at Connecticut Avenue. This trail is usually a better route if the tunnel is muddy. The path then leaves the creek and crosses Beach Drive, then crosses Kensington Parkway and stays parallel to Beach Drive until you reach mile 3.

There is an all-weather water fountain on the left after the marker for mile 3. The path then crosses Beach Drive again and continues between Beach Drive and the creek, offering views of the imposing white and gold spires of the Washington Mormon Temple. It then goes under the Capital Beltway and crosses Jones Mill Road before entering a woody secluded area just past a small playground that takes you to the mile-2 marker.

After a hilly wooded section you cross under the historic Rock Creek Railroad Trestle that was built in 1892. This bridge is slated to become part of the northern section of the Capital Crescent Trail, connecting the Rock Creek path to the C&O Towpath (see Capital Crescent routes in this section). After you pass under the trestle, the path enters Ray's Meadow Park, then crosses the East West Highway at a light before you come to Meadowbrook Park and the stables at the mile-1 marker.

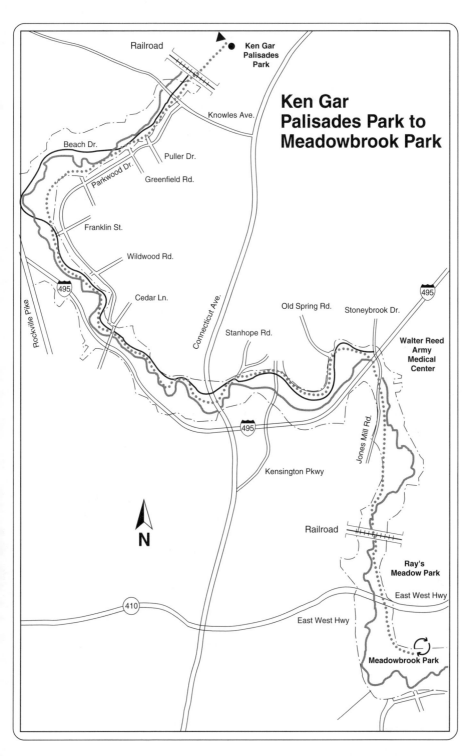

Ken Gar
Palisades Park to
Meadowbrook Park

Railroad

Ken Gar
Palisades
Park

Knowles Ave.

Beach Dr.

Puller Dr.

Parkwood Dr.

Greenfield Rd.

Franklin St.

Wildwood Rd.

495

Cedar Ln.

Rockville Pike

Old Spring Rd.

Stoneybrook Dr.

495

Connecticut Ave.

Stanhope Rd.

Walter Reed
Army
Medical
Center

495

Jones Mill Rd.

Kensington Pkwy

N

Railroad

Ray's
Meadow Park

East West Hwy

410

East West Hwy

Meadowbrook Park

FOUR-MILE RUN WEST—
WASHINGTON & OLD DOMINION
TRAIL–CUSTIS TRAIL

3.3-7 MILES	TRAIL	SCENERY RATING	
		HILL RATING	

ACCESS

The midpoint of the measured section of Four-Mile Run can be reached by car from exit 71 on Route 66 (Glebe Road exit, Route 120). From the west, take a right onto Glebe Road, then another right onto Wilson Boulevard; from the east, of course, take a left onto Glebe Road. Go south on Wilson Boulevard for just under a mile and a half. Just past Lexington Street, you'll see lots for two parks—Bluemont Park to your left, and Bon Air Park and Rose Garden on the right. The trail runs through both and is clearly visible.

Choose a lot according to which route you're running. If you're heading west, you'll start from Bon Air Park. If you're going east, park in the Bluemont lot.

It is possible to get to the trailhead by Metro, but the options are a bit more limited. The East Falls Church Metro stop is across the highway from East Falls Church Park, which marks the beginning of the western end of both the Custis Trail and Four-Mile Run.

COURSE

Four-Mile Run is something of a misnomer—the real length of the trail that runs east-west from the Falls Church–Arlington border through Alexandria to the Mount Vernon Trail is closer to 8 miles. The trail is a favorite among D.C. runners, especially in the western section, which passes through many small, lovely parks. The eastern half is more industrial, especially from Route 395 to the Mount Vernon Trail.

For Washington novices, the various trail intersections and mile markers can be a bit confusing. Four-Mile run begins to the west as part

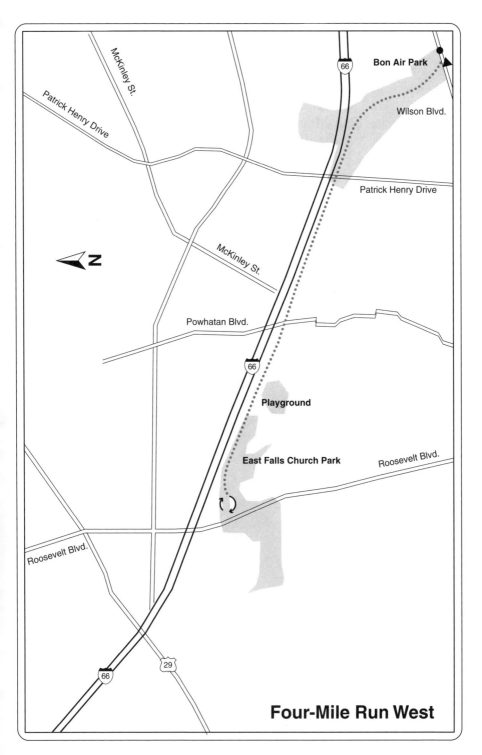

Four-Mile Run West

of the Custis Trail, then runs in tandem with the Washington & Old Dominion Trail for most of the rest of the way, with adjacent mileage markers for all three trails posted at various points. There is, however, a one-way measured 4-mile section of Four-Mile Run that extends from the Custis Trail in Falls Church to George Mason Drive in Arlington.

Here, then, is Four-Mile Run simplified, with two out-and-back runs that start close to the middle of the measured section, although neither is *exactly* 4 miles.

This western section of the trail is the lesser of the two options, in both distance and scenery. It starts with a pleasant stretch through Bon Air Park that brings you alongside Route 66; a tall concrete embankment shields you from the highway. After a small but fairly steep hill, the trail winds to the left toward East Falls Church Park. At this point the Four-Mile Run trail runs in parallel with the Custis Trail.

East Falls Church Park is the turnaround point, although it's possible to continue for many miles on the Washington & Old Dominion Trail to the west, or break off along the Custis Trail to the east, which eventually leads back to the Arlington Memorial Bridge.

FOUR-MILE RUN EAST— BLUEMONT PARK TO BARCROFT PARK

1.8 MILES	ROAD/TRAIL 🚻 💧 🎵	SCENERY RATING					
		HILL RATING					

ACCESS

To drive, follow the directions for the Four-Mile Run West. Park in the Bluemont lot to run the east route.

COURSE

This stretch of Four-Mile Run offers the best scenery, passing through several pleasant parks within a short stretch. Shortly after the start at Bluemont Park the trail separates into upper and lower sections at Glen Carlyn Park, after which you'll pass the Long Branch Nature Center.

From there the run continues to South George Mason Drive and the beginning of Barcroft Park, which marks the official 4-mile turnaround point (if you want to continue, the Four-Mile Run–Bike Path starts here). Another possible turnaround point is the underpass about a half mile shy of George Mason Drive, which turns you around and puts you on the opposite side of the road at Columbia Pike. After Barcroft Park, however, the character of the run becomes decidedly more industrial.

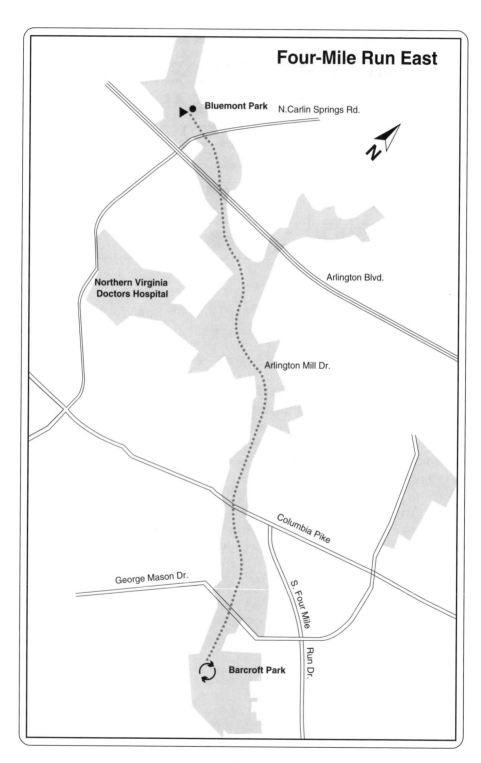

Four-Mile Run East

Bluemont Park

N.Carlin Springs Rd.

Northern Virginia
Doctors Hospital

Arlington Blvd.

Arlington Mill Dr.

Columbia Pike

George Mason Dr.

S. Four Mile

Run Dr.

Barcroft Park

CAPITAL CRESCENT TRAIL, NORTHERN SECTION (BETHESDA TO MASSACHUSETTS AVENUE)

5-6 MILES	TRAIL	SCENERY RATING	
		HILL RATING	

Complementing the extensive network of trails offered by Rock Creek Park Trail, the Capital Crescent Trail meets the getaway needs of D.C. denizens and Maryland residents in Montgomery County. The trail runs along part of the stretch from the Key Bridge in Georgetown toward the Chain Bridge, breaking north toward Bethesda Center just before the Chain Bridge.

This trail is one of the more successful examples of the highly regarded rails-to-trails program in which recreational and commuting resources have replaced tracks and trains. This trail traces the route of the old Georgetown Spur, a B&O Railroad line from Georgetown to Silver Spring that was completed in 1910 and used until 1985.

ACCESS

From the northern half of the Beltway, take exit 34 south and follow Wisconsin Avenue into downtown Bethesda. You'll come to a series of large retail stores; look for a large parking lot where Hampden Road meets Wisconsin Avenue. Just behind this parking lot next to a large car dealership you'll see the beginning of the trail.

By Metro, the Bethesda stop leaves you just north of Hampden Road on Wisconsin. Keep in mind, however, that if you're going to do a one-way run and use the Metro to get back, you'll have to run all the way down the trail past the Key Bridge to the beginning of Rock Creek Park, where you can head over to the Foggy Bottom station to return to Bethesda.

COURSE

The upper half of the Capital Crescent Trail is easier to get to than the lower, but it's definitely the lesser of the two halves in scenery. The first mile or so south of Bethesda is industrial in character, and it isn't until the Little Falls Parkway intersection that the trail begins to display its more peaceful side, surrounding runners and cyclists with greenery.

After that, though, it's a very pleasant run, with several convenient turnaround points along the more than 5-mile stretch that takes you to the Fletcher Boathouse, where the Capital Crescent then runs parallel with the C&O Towpath. The River Road trail crosses the Capital Crescent at approximately the 2.2-mile mark, and the Massachusetts Avenue crossover constitutes the midpoint for a 5-mile out-and-back from Bethesda.

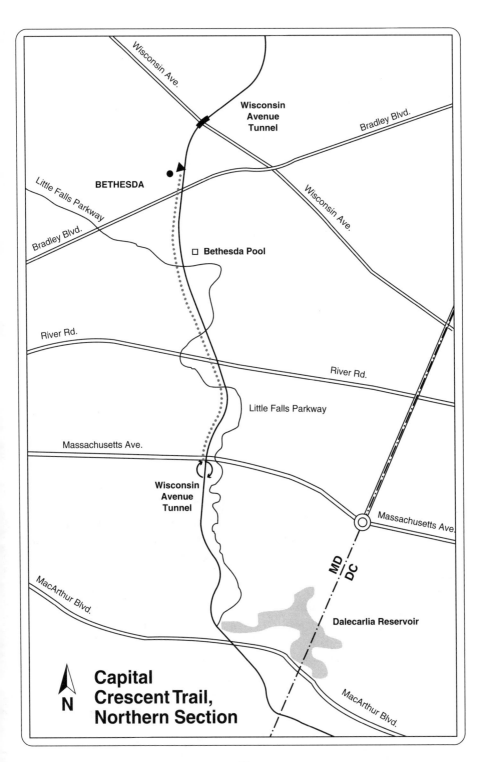

**Capital
Crescent Trail,
Northern Section**

CAPITAL CRESCENT TRAIL, SOUTHERN SECTION (MASSACHUSETTS AVENUE TO C&O TOWPATH)

5-6 MILES 👫 💧 ☎	TRAIL	SCENERY RATING	🌳 🌳 🌳 🌳
		HILL RATING	⛰ ⛰

ACCESS

There are two access points for a southern start on the Capital Crescent Trail—the beginning of the trail at the Key Bridge or the Fletcher Boathouse parking area on the C&O Towpath. These directions assume a start from the Fletcher Boathouse, which you can reach from Canal Road by a left turn that you can make only if you're going *west*.

COURSE

While this particular section of the trail offers no mass-transit access, it is easy to connect to other trails, and it gets you into the good scenery early in the run. From the boathouse, cross the narrow wooden bridge to get to the towpath, then head beyond the towpath to the macadam path. Take a right onto this path, and within a half mile you'll come to and cross the trestle bridge over Canal Road that is one of the showcase features of this trail.

After the trestle bridge the trail winds north and breaks away from the river; you'll get a glimpse of the Chain Bridge as the trail curves. The next major landmark is the water tower in the midst of the Defense Mapping Agency, a group of buildings surrounded by barbed wire in the middle of the Dalecarlia Reservoir Grounds.

From there you have your choice of the same three turnaround points in the northern half: the River Road crossing point, the Massachusetts Avenue crossing point, or the Little Falls Parkway crossover point. Or you can go to the end and shop till you drop.

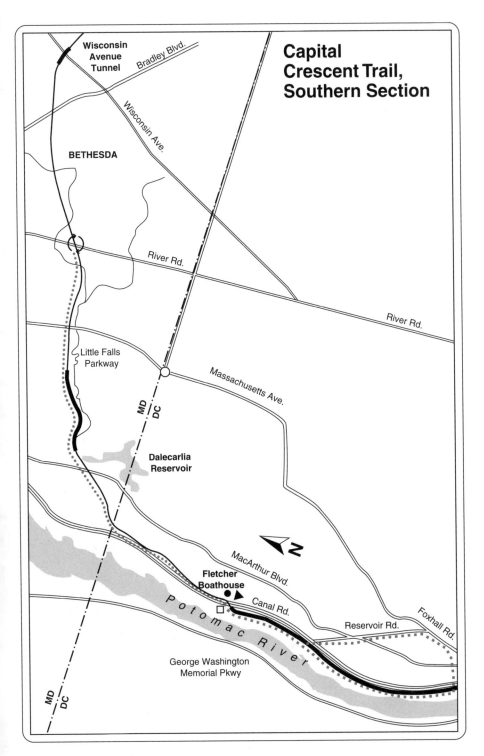

Capital
Crescent Trail,
Southern Section

Wisconsin
Avenue
Tunnel

Bradley Blvd.

Wisconsin Ave.

BETHESDA

River Rd.

River Rd.

Little Falls
Parkway

Massachusetts Ave.

MD | DC

Dalecarlia
Reservoir

N

MacArthur Blvd.

Fletcher
Boathouse

Canal Rd.

Foxhall Rd.

Reservoir Rd.

Potomac River

George Washington
Memorial Pkwy

MD | DC

EXTENSIONS

If you go west from the Fletcher Boathouse, you can also skip the trestle bridge and stay on the Chesapeake & Ohio Towpath, from which you can either cross the Chain Bridge or continue and almost run a marathon. You can also head east back toward the Key Bridge for approximately 2 miles, then take the underpass to Glover Archbold Park just before Foxhall Road breaks off Canal Road (see the section on running in downtown), or you can return to the Key Bridge and do one of the downtown runs.

CENTRAL MOUNT VERNON TRAIL (DAINGERFIELD ISLAND TO ALEXANDRIA)

5-6 MILES	TRAIL 👫 💧 ☕	SCENERY RATING	🌳🌳🌳🌳
		HILL RATING	

ACCESS

You can park for this run at either Daingerfield Island or Old Town Alexandria; each site has tradeoffs. The Daingerfield Island exit is marked from the highway if you're going north on the George Washington Memorial Parkway from Alexandria or Mount Vernon, but you'll have to turn around to use this exit if you're coming from downtown. There's plenty of parking at the north end of Old Town Alexandria, but you'll have to drive through the downtown area, which is full of traffic lights, and many of the access highways aren't too direct.

You can also run this route as a one-way using mass transit from the Eisenhower Avenue Metro station, but it will add another mile to the route, and you'll have to run along a bike path through a run-down, industrial section of south Alexandria to get to an isolated Metro station. Directions are as follows:

From the Metro station, head east (right out of the station) on Eisenhower for a half mile across a small bridge; take a hard right and look for the bike trail, which curls around some warehouses and factories and leaves you on Payne Street. Follow Payne Street south to Franklin, take a right, and run east for approximately a half mile; when you come to the end you'll be within a quarter mile of the starting point in Old Town.

Finally, you can also park at Belle Haven in the middle of the route using the exit from the southbound side of the George Washington Memorial Parkway.

COURSE

The central section of the Mount Vernon Trail offers a variety of scenic and historic attractions; the problem is that in many cases they're located too far apart to lend themselves to a single out-and-back loop of reasonable length. This run solves that problem by skipping the relatively grungy section along National Airport for a 5.5- to 6-mile run from Daingerfield Island along the waterfront, then through historic Old Town Alexandria.

Daingerfield Island is a small but pleasant marina on 107 acres of land just to the south of the 12-mile mark on the Mount Vernon Trail. As you approach the 11-mile mark, the road bends toward the Potomac, and just before you enter Alexandria proper it breaks toward the waterfront for a stretch that's especially appealing at sunset. There are several slightly tricky breaks in the trail as you head toward Old Town, but the bike path is generally well marked along Union Street through Old Town, and it's difficult to get lost in the congested grid of downtown Alexandria.

Old Town, however, is a much more appealing section—a historic district dating to 1749 with narrow, red-brick sidewalks and cobblestone streets and an architectural approach that maintains a unique charm without advertising the area's status as a tourist attraction. The turnaround point for this run is easily recognizable as you approach the end of Old Town; just beyond Old Town you'll pass Jones Point Lighthouse (which was named after a beaver trader who built his cabin there in 1692; it was once used to warn passing ships of sandbars), with views of the Woodrow Wilson Bridge over the Potomac River. Following the bike route signs parallel to the bridge leads you back to the bike path heading south toward Mount Vernon.

OTHER OPTIONS

For a more naturalistic run in the central section of the Mount Vernon Trail, you can start from Belle Haven, a popular picnic spot located just north of the 7-mile mark, which was once a settlement of Scottish merchants that sprang up around a tobacco warehouse. If you start by heading north on this 4-mile out-and-back, you'll go through some marshes and mudflats just south of Hunting Creek with a view of the Woodrow Wilson Bridge. To the south, you run on trails and boardwalks past and through the 240-acre Dyke Marsh, a section of wetlands that's popular among local bird-watchers.

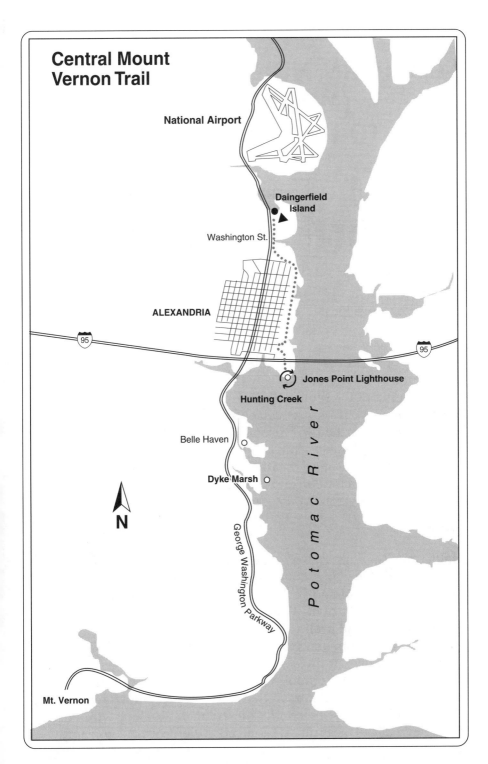

Central Mount Vernon Trail

National Airport

Daingerfield Island

Washington St.

ALEXANDRIA

95

95

Jones Point Lighthouse

Hunting Creek

Belle Haven

Dyke Marsh

N

Potomac River

George Washington Parkway

Mt. Vernon

SOUTHERN MOUNT VERNON TRAIL (MOUNT VERNON TO FORT HUNT PARK)

6 MILES	TRAIL 👫 💧 ☎	SCENERY RATING	🌳🌳🌳🌳🌳
		HILL RATING	

ACCESS

Mount Vernon is located 16 miles from downtown Washington near the Potomac just off the George Washington Parkway. This trail can be reached by several roads, including Route 495 and Route 95 to the northeast or northwest, and Route 1 directly from the north or south. The George Washington Parkway takes you into a rotary that marks the beginning of the Mount Vernon property—you'll see the Mount Vernon Inn on your right as you enter.

When you enter the rotary from the George Washington Parkway, there are two parking lots, one on your left just as you enter the rotary, the other halfway around the rotary opposite the Mount Vernon Inn. The trail begins on the end of the lot farthest from the inn, which is off to the left (northwest) if you're facing the lot from the inn itself.

COURSE

Unlike many of Washington's bike trails, the Mount Vernon Trail offers completely different highlights in each section of the path. This particular run, a 6-mile out-and-back along the first 3 miles of the trail, offers some pristine views of the Potomac as it flows into Chesapeake Bay.

Although the trail itself winds along the George Washington Parkway, this route is anything but a highway run. Although you never quite get far enough from the road to escape the traffic noise, the initial stretches of the trail are shrouded in woods before the middle section opens up to offer the Potomac views. After a steep downhill section, gentle, rolling hills are present for most of the way, along with stops in a couple small but pleasant parks and great views of the Potomac River.

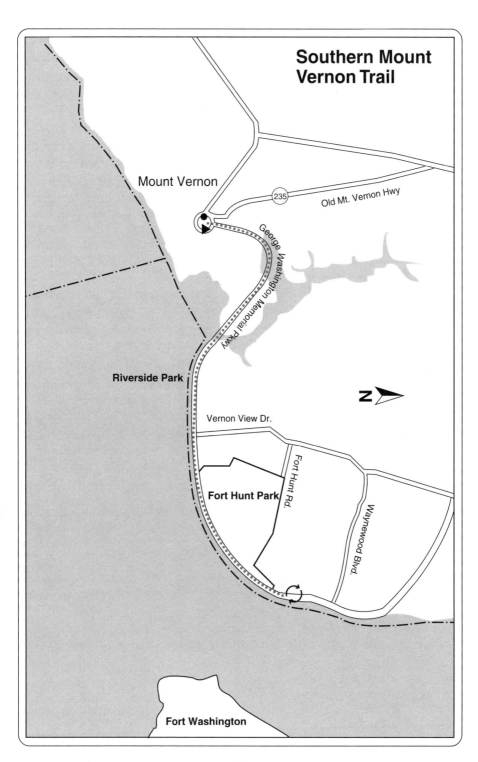

Southern Mount Vernon Trail

Mount Vernon

235 Old Mt. Vernon Hwy

George Washington Memorial Pkwy

Riverside Park

Vernon View Dr.

Fort Hunt Rd.

Fort Hunt Park

Waynewood Blvd.

N

Fort Washington

The first of these is Riverside Park, a picnic spot just north of Little Hunting Creek at the 1-mile mark. After you leave this park there's a fitness course on the trail; the next landmark is the 156-acre Fort Hunt Park just beyond the 2-mile mark. For variety you can also take the half-mile loop around the park, and you can use the parking lot here if you're interested in starting from the northern end of the trail.

Almost all of the trail is sufficiently isolated from the highway to minimize any safety concerns, but you should use some caution at the underpass just before the northern entrance to Fort Hunt Park. There's little traffic here, but the trail almost disappears for approximately 50 yards when you go through the underpass, so you'll want to keep well to the sides if you hear cars nearby.

NORTHEAST BRANCH– NORTHWEST BRANCH TRAILS (WITH METRO CONNECTOR)

5 MILES	TRAIL ◐ ℂ	SCENERY RATING	
		HILL RATING	

ACCESS

You can start this Metro run from either the College Park station or the West Hyattsville stop. If you're driving to College Park, take exit 23 from the Beltway to Route 201 south and drive 2 miles to Paint Branch Parkway (also labeled on some maps as either Calvert Road or Good Luck Road) and take a right. (If you take a left here, you'll be at the southern starting point for the Greenbelt Park run.) The Metro station will be on your left after a mile; both metered and daily parking are available.

To get to the West Hyattsville station, take Route 29 south (Colesville Road) from exit 30 off the Beltway. Drive for a half mile and take a left onto Sligo Creek Parkway, then continue for approximately 2.5 miles to the intersection of the parkway and New Hampshire Avenue. Take a right onto New Hampshire then a left onto Ethan Allen Avenue, which becomes the East West Highway (Route 410). Follow this road for approximately 1.5 miles, then take the fork to the right to Ager Road, which takes you to the Metro station.

If you're getting to this run by Metro, both stops are on the Green Line, which extends from Union Station downtown to the Greenbelt station just inside the northeast section of the Beltway.

COURSE

Those desperate for flat terrain will find much to love about this pleasant but somewhat nondescript journey from the College Park Metro station to its West Hyattsville counterpart. The crescent-shaped 5-mile route connects the Northeast and Northwest Branch Trails.

Although it has a suburban-industrial flavor to it, the fast course covers both branches of the Anacostia River, taking you through some decent park space along the way.

You can start the run from either Metro station, but College Park is the better bet for both convenience and safety. As you leave the station, look for the Paint Branch Parkway, which curves along to the right. Run along the Paint Branch for a quarter mile until you come to the Denis Wolf rest station, which is also the starting point for the Lake Artemesia route. Take a right at the rest station and pick up the trail.

You'll pass through several generic parks before the only tricky part of this run, the link between the Northeast and Northwest Branch Trail. Just after you pass under the railroad bridge around the 2-mile mark, you'll come to Baltimore Avenue, a major secondary road; take the fork to the right up to Baltimore Avenue, cross the road, and take the unmarked road that is actually Charles L. Armentrout Place just to the right of the overpass. Stay on the sidewalk to the left for just under a quarter mile and cross Rhode Island Avenue, where you can pick up the trail across the street. Follow it to the left through a playground and then a small park until you come to the Northwest Branch Trail, which breaks off to the right.

You'll cross the river on this trail about a half mile before the end of the run. There's a footbridge off to the right just before Queens Chapel Road, which marks the continuation of the trail to Sligo Creek. Instead follow the macadam path, cross Queens Chapel Road, and take the unmarked road directly across from the path that leads into the West Hyattsville station parking lot. (Exercise caution; this isn't a great area.)

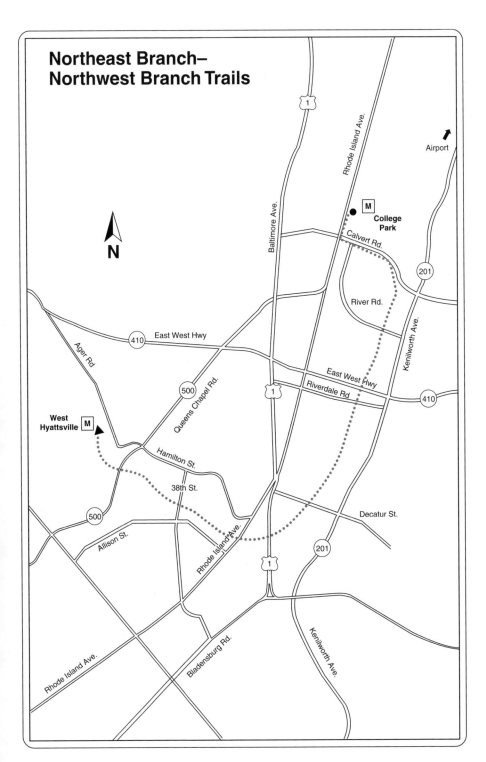

Northeast Branch–
Northwest Branch Trails

N

Airport

Rhode Island Ave.

Baltimore Ave.

M College
Park

Calvert Rd.

River Rd.

East West Hwy

Ager Rd

East West Hwy

Riverdale Rd

Kenilworth Ave.

Queens Chapel Rd.

West
Hyattsville M

Hamilton St.

38th St.

Decatur St.

Allison St.

Rhode Island Ave.

Rhode Island Ave.

Bladensburg Rd.

Kenilworth Ave.

LAKE ARTEMESIA

4 MILES	TRAIL	SCENERY RATING	🌲🌲🌲
		HILL RATING	⛰

ACCESS

From the Beltway, take exit 25 to Route 1 south. Go on for just under 2 miles, then take a left onto the Paint Branch Parkway. About a quarter mile past the College Park Metro station, Paint Branch Parkway merges with Calvert Road; look for the Denis Wolf rest station on your right and park in the small lot.

If you're going by Metro, take a right out of the College Park Metro station and go approximately a quarter mile to the Denis Wolf rest station.

COURSE

Sick of running along meandering streams and babbling brooks? That, along with the relative absence of lake loops in the metro D.C. area, is as good a reason as any to run this pleasant, 4-mile out-and-back run that starts along the upper section of the Northeast Branch Trail, then shifts to the Indian Creek Trail along Artemesia Lake before the turnaround point at Indian Creek Park.

The course starts with a left at the Denis Wolf rest station, which takes you beneath Calvert Road. At this point the trail breaks sharply to the left; you'll have a tributary of the Anacostia River on your right until the trail curves left and takes you past a small airfield to the obvious left turn to Lake Artemesia. This lake is a pleasant but innocuous body of water, with the setting marred only by the Metro tracks on the opposite shore that come into view when you first reach the gate.

For variety, you can run out along the shore of the lake on the right-hand side and visit the opposite side on the way back, or you can take as many lake loops as you like. The shoreline is approximately 0.6 miles in length on the right, after which you'll go through a gate and then the postage-stamp-size Artemesia Lake Park.

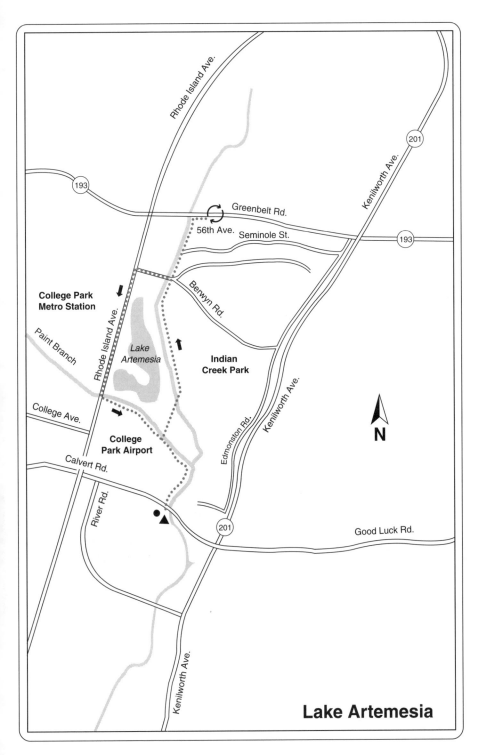

Lake Artemesia

At the corner of the park, take a right onto Berwyn Road, then run for a very short block and take a left onto the Indian Creek Trail. The trail meanders along the river through the generic suburban edge of Berwyn Heights until it ends at Indian Creek Park. When it ends you'll be facing the intersection of Greenbelt Road (Route 193) and Branchville Road, which marks the beginning of a large four-lane highway with a series of busy strip malls that is unmistakably the turnaround point.

The Metro side of the lake on the way back offers a bit more variety. If you stick to the outer trail the distance is about the same as on the way out, but there's also a shorter loop that hugs the shore of the lake and brings you to a wooden bridge that is a more direct route to the trail back along the river.

SLIGO CREEK TRAIL SOUTH– LONG BRANCH LOOP

5.0 MILES	TRAIL ◐ ☏	SCENERY RATING	🌲 🌲 🌲		
		HILL RATING	⛰️⛰️		

ACCESS

This run begins where two branches of the Sligo Creek Trail meet at New Hampshire Avenue in Takoma Park. If you're facing Sligo Creek Parkway from New Hampshire Avenue, the western branch starts to the left and runs along Sligo Creek Parkway. Farther to the right of this starting point there's a barrier; the Long Branch section of the trail starts just to the right of the barrier.

COURSE

The Sligo Creek Trail is one of several trails north of the city that run parallel to one another toward the Beltway. The trail sits between the Rock Creek Park Trail and the Northwest Branch Trail; this triangular route traces a section of the trail that runs through Takoma Park.

Variety is what makes this run worthwhile. You can run the Long Branch section of the trail as a 5-mile out-and-back, or cut over on one of several avenues to run back on the western branch of the trail.

That sense of variety also extends to the Long Branch section, which offers both a dirt trail with several challenging creek crossings and the macadam bike path that runs parallel to Piney Branch Road. The first section is the trickiest; after you run past a playground the trail becomes tight and narrow, and you must cross the creek to reach the first major street crossing at Carroll Avenue.

Much of this trail has the feel of a blue-collar run through the woods—small brick houses line the trail throughout, and there are several points at which it veers perilously close to the occasional backyard. As of this writing, Takoma Park was struggling with a bit of a crime problem, evidence of which could be found in the "No

Trespassing" signs and crime-watch notifications along the way, a sure sign that you should exercise caution.

LOOP POSSIBILITIES

If you want to run this route as a loop, there are two major cutovers. The first is at Carroll Avenue, in a residential section at the 0.75-mile mark. The cutover adds just over 0.25 mile, making for a very quick loop of just under 2 miles. The second is at Piney Branch Avenue at the 1.75-mile mark; with the cutover the total distance is just under 4 miles. If you want to extend the distance once you're on the western branch, you can run well past the Beltway on this branch of the Sligo Creek Trail.

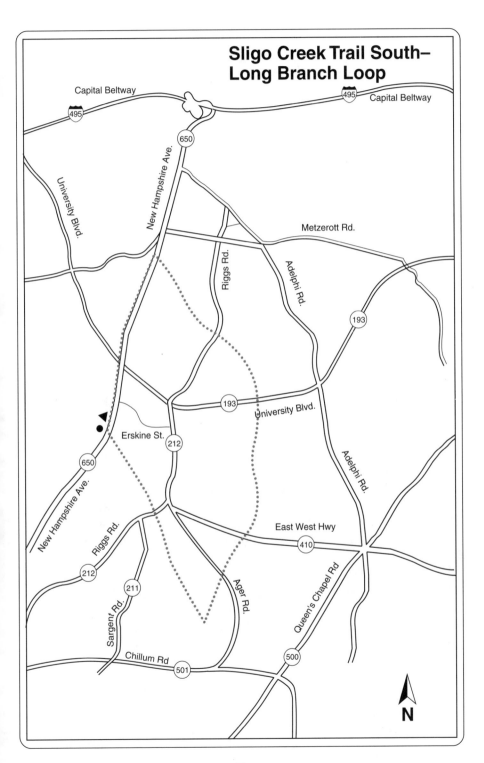

Sligo Creek Trail South–
Long Branch Loop

GREENBELT PARK

5.5- 6.5 MILES	TRAIL	SCENERY RATING	
		HILL RATING	

ACCESS

Greenbelt Park can be reached by exit 23 from the Beltway. For the 5.5-mile loop, follow Route 201 south from the exit for approximately a half mile, then make a left onto Route 193 heading east. After another quarter mile you'll see the park headquarters sign off to the right of Walker Drive; the state police also occupy several buildings here, which can make parking scarce.

Parking at the south end of the park adds distance, but more spaces are available. To get to this lot, continue south on Route 201 past Route 193 for approximately two miles to the traffic light at the Paint Branch Parkway. Take a left and you'll soon be on Good Luck Road. In just under a mile you'll see the parking area on your left. The gate closes at dusk, so if you're running in late afternoon or early evening you may want to register your vehicle with the park rangers back up at the northern end.

It's also possible to get to this run by mass transit from the College Park Metro station. Head right out of the station onto Calvert Road–Paint Branch Parkway until it changes to Good Luck Road, and after approximately a mile and a half you'll come to the south gate.

COURSE

The primary loop in Greenbelt Park is the 5.5-mile Bridle Trail, a 2-mile long, 0.5-mile wide oval loop that runs north and south, hugging the park perimeter on the east side. This description assumes a southern start—if you're running from the north end, the loop (which was undergoing some restoration work as of this writing) starts from the end of the parking lot and heads west for approximately a half mile before breaking south.

One of the advantages of a counterclockwise southern start is that it gets the stretches along the highway over with early in the run. Run

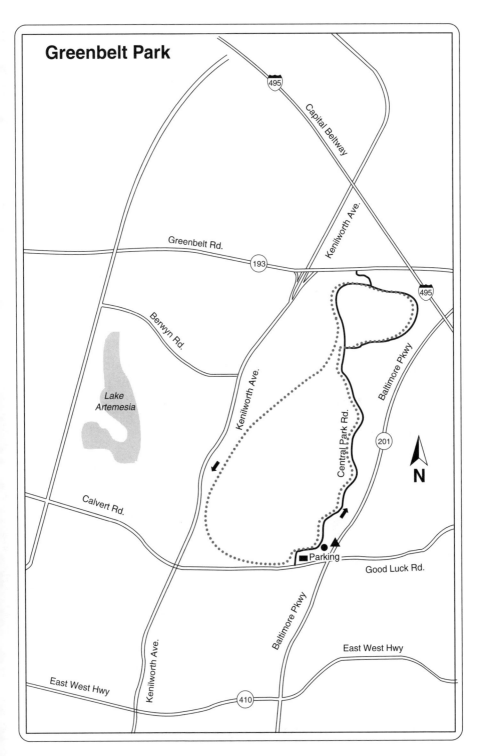

Greenbelt Park

Lake
Artemesia

Parking

495

Capital Beltway

Kenilworth Ave.

Greenbelt Rd.

193

Berwyn Rd.

Kenilworth Ave.

Baltimore Pkwy

Central Park Rd.

201

N

Calvert Rd.

Good Luck Rd.

Baltimore Pkwy

Kenilworth Ave.

East West Hwy

East West Hwy

410

along the macadam road that extends for a half mile from the parking lot until you get to a chain-link fence, where you'll see trail markers to your right and left. This is the Bridle Trail, which is marked by single and double yellow markers that periodically seem to split before coming back together again.

Take a right at the fence and get ready for some fairly steep hills. You'll be able to see both Route 193 and the Beltway as the trail curves along the northern edge of the park. When you come to the park headquarters, continue to the end of the parking lot and pick up the restored section just beyond the police trailer.

The next stretch south through the center of the park is the payoff on this run. The hills get gentler, and although you'll have the occasional view of an apartment complex along the western perimeter, you're in the woods for the most part. Back at the south end you'll come within hailing distance of Good Luck Road before the trail turns back toward the center of the park.

There are two spots where you can break from the trail. The official end is back at the chain-link fence, where you can take a right and run the macadam road back to the lot. If you're in need of a shortcut, look for the macadam road when you come to a set of wooden slats that takes you over a swamp. From there it's a quick right to get back to the road, which saves a tenth of a mile or two.

WAKEFIELD PARK, LAKE ACCOTINK

6 MILES	TRAIL	SCENERY RATING	
	🚻 💧 ☕	HILL RATING	

ACCESS

To get to Wakefield Park, take exit 5 from the southwestern section of the Beltway. Follow Route 620 (Braddock Road) west, and within a half mile you'll see the park on your left. Park in the first of the two parking lots; the trailhead is at the end of this lot.

COURSE

Many runs in Washington meander along streams and rivers, but few offer the combination of lake and river access provided by this 6-mile loop around Lake Accotink. It's also a psychologically satisfying course, opening up into a series of fine lake views after a long stretch along a typical Washington stream. The trail is flat and fast, albeit occasionally muddy, with one steep hill just short of the 2-mile mark on the way out.

The starting point is Wakefield Park, a modest facility with a baseball field in front of the two main parking lots. The trail begins from the east end of the lot, then immediately bends hard to the right to pick up the stream. After 0.8 miles you'll come to a right turn that leads across a small bridge. Cross the bridge and follow the trail until you come to the staircase that leads up to Danbury Forest Road. Stay on the trail and remain to the left. The trail will hug the shoreline for the next mile, with the river on your left.

This section of the trail is tight and narrow but quite runnable, although you should avoid it during heavy rains. At the 1.8-mile mark you'll come to a small creek that breaks off to the right. Cross the creek and follow the shoreline, then climb a steep hill and pick up the trail, which runs along a ridge. After 50 yards or so the trail breaks sharply downhill to the right, leading into a wide dirt road labeled as Marina

Drive on the chain-link fence where you first pick it up. This road runs along the south end of the lake and brings you to the dam.

If the conditions are muddy, climb the staircase to Danbury Forest Road and go straight up a hill and past a school on the right. As you come down the hill, look for a red arrow pointing to the right down a flight of stairs, after which you'll cross a small creek. Follow this path for a few hundred feet until you come to a right turn that leads back to the Wakefield Park path.

When you get to the dam, cross the water in front of it and follow the shoreline past the refreshment stand, where you'll see a wooden bridge off to the left that leads to the return path. At this point you'll be on the Lake Accotink Trail, which is marked by either red or green blazes. Houses are off to the right, and the stream will now be on your left. Just after you come to the bridge you crossed on the way out, the trail will break right and then left, returning you to the parking lot at Wakefield Park.

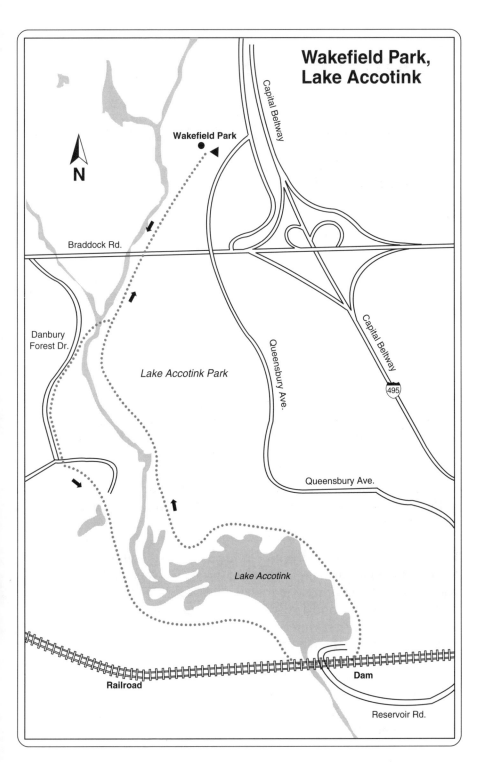

Wakefield Park, Lake Accotink

N

Capital Beltway

Wakefield Park

Braddock Rd.

Danbury Forest Dr.

Lake Accotink Park

Queensbury Ave.

Capital Beltway

495

Queensbury Ave.

Lake Accotink

Railroad

Dam

Reservoir Rd.

PATUXENT WILDLIFE REFUGE

3.5 MILES 👫 💧 🕯	ROAD/TRAIL	SCENERY RATING	🌳 🌳 🌳 🌳 🌳
		HILL RATING	

ACCESS

To get to the Patuxent Wildlife Refuge, take exit 22 north onto the Baltimore–Washington Parkway (Route 295). Follow Route 295 north for 3.4 miles, then take the Powder Mill Road–Beltsville exit. At the end of the ramp, you'll see signs pointing to the right for the National Wildlife Visitor Center. Go 2 miles on Powder Mill Road, then make a right at the gate and follow the one-way road to the Visitor Center, which has plenty of parking.

COURSE

This 3.5-mile loop with a short out-and-back section is a guaranteed "critter run"—it's almost impossible to do this route without seeing at least a half-dozen white-tailed deer, sometimes within the first quarter mile. The runnable section described here comprises a minute fraction of the 12,750-acre Patuxent Research Refuge, which is run by the U.S. Fish and Wildlife Service. Runners are welcome, but you'll have to stick to the marked trails and run between 10:00 A.M. and 5:30 P.M. when the Visitor Center is open.

If you're standing at the Visitor Center facing the end of the parking lot, head straight out to the end of the lot, where you'll find the Fire Road Trail, which arcs off to your left (west) and then gradually veers back toward Telegraph Road for 0.9 miles. Cross Telegraph Road and pick up the Goose Pond Trail, which extends for another 0.6 miles and brings you to the first water view.

When you reach the water, pick up the Cash Lake Trail and run the 0.2-mile extension to the pier. If you keep going down the cinder track past the end of the pier, you'll see another trail that will eventually lead to a bridge extending across Cash Lake. Turn back, head along the shoreline, and pick up the Loop Trail, which will take you to the Goose Pond Trail and then back to the Visitor Center.

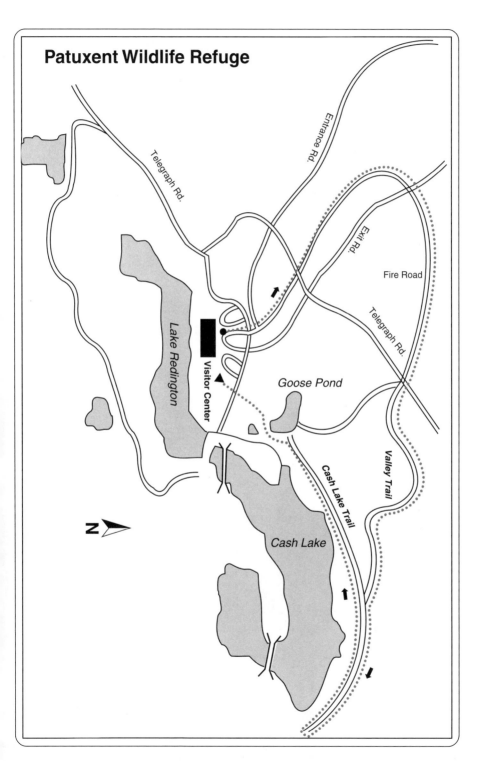

Patuxent Wildlife Refuge

Telegraph Rd.

Entrance Rd.

Exit Rd.

Fire Road

Telegraph Rd.

Lake Redington

Visitor Center

Goose Pond

Cash Lake Trail

Valley Trail

Cash Lake

N

The initial trails through the woods are wide and well marked, although the distance markers at the various trailheads seem suspiciously short. Cash Lake is especially beautiful at sunset, and the final macadam path leads directly into the side-rear entrance of the Visitor Center, which contains several excellent exhibits and a gift shop and offers tram tours.

EXTENSIONS

For the truly ambitious trail runner, a much larger section of the refuge called the North Tract is open for running just south of Fort Meade, not far from the next exit north off the parkway for Route 198. For a map, hours, and specific trail routes, call 410-674-3304.

BATTLEFIELD PARK, STONE BRIDGE TRAIL

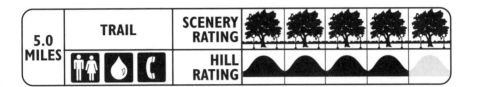

5.0 MILES	TRAIL	SCENERY RATING	
	👫 💧 📞	HILL RATING	

ACCESS

Battlefield Park is located just over 20 miles from downtown Washington. Take Route 66 from either the city or the Beltway (exit 12). Follow Route 66 to exit 47B and then follow signs for Battlefield Park, located just past the Northern Virginia Community College Manassas Campus on Route 234 north. Park in the Visitor Center lot, but make sure you pay the $2 park admission fee or you'll get slapped with a $30 fine.

COURSE

Few running routes have universal appeal, but this 5-mile loop through the rolling hills of northern Virginia really does offer something for everyone. History buffs, of course, will delight in the tour of the Bull Run battle site. The course is full of descriptive markers explaining the significance of the various locations with quotations from both Union and Confederate soldiers who participated in the battle.

The park also functions as a *de facto* nature preserve, offering glimpses of deer, grouse, a variety of birds, and an occasional fox in the small hours of the morning. Finally, this course has many attractions and challenges as a running route. The first 2 miles make for a fast, flat cross-country route, while the second half offers enough hills to challenge even veteran trail runners.

The Stone Bridge Trail is one of two longer loops through the park that start from the Visitor Center. If you're facing the statue of Stonewall Jackson in front of the center, you will find the trail marker at the quarter-mile mark between the third and fourth cannons in the row of seven cannons that stand just beyond Stonewall's grim visage.

The trail, marked by a blue dot, passes eight marked historical stops. For 50 cents you can buy a Manassas Battlefield Walking Tour map that describes the trail. A free Manassas brochure shows all the trails, although it supplies a bit too much detail and occasionally fails to outline adequately the path of the Stone Bridge Trail.

Although the trail itself is relatively well marked, several turns can be tricky because of the abundance of bridle paths. The first is the left turn just after Jackson's guns around the first mile—avoid the angular right that will take you to the edge of the park. Similarly, proceed with caution when crossing the Warrenton Turnpike shortly thereafter—the two-lane highway carries fast-moving traffic.

The next junction where you'll want to be careful is just after Farm Ford along the Bull Run River. Here the trail breaks left away from the river, and within a tenth of a mile or so there's a sign for the next two attractions, the Pittsylvania Cemetery and the Stovall Marker. Make sure you take the sharp right, otherwise it's easy to wind up back at the Van Pelt House ruins (stop 2).

The hills through this section are challenging, but the last mile and a half is especially delightful, taking you up and down the long fields, past huge rolled bales of hay, and cannons that mark the various strategic positions.

Several caveats regarding weather and critters are necessary. Summer hazards include ticks and mosquitoes, and during winter ice can be especially cruel. Rainy stretches turn the red clay into a slick, gooey mass that glues itself to running shoes.

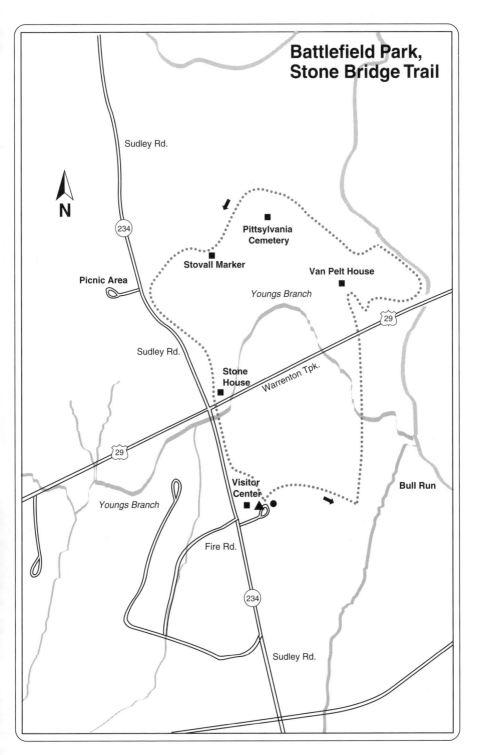

Battlefield Park, Stone Bridge Trail

N

Sudley Rd.

234

Picnic Area

Sudley Rd.

Pittsylvania Cemetery

Stovall Marker

Van Pelt House

Youngs Branch

29

Stone House

Warrenton Tpk.

29

Youngs Branch

Visitor Center

Fire Rd.

Bull Run

234

Sudley Rd.

CHESAPEAKE & OHIO (C&O) CANAL TOWPATH, GREAT FALLS PARK

4.2+ MILES	TRAIL	SCENERY RATING	🌳🌳🌳🌳
	🚹🚺 💧 ☎	HILL RATING	⛰️⛰️⛰️

ACCESS

From the Beltway, take exit 41 for the Clara Barton Parkway, which hugs the river and eventually becomes MacArthur Boulevard. The entrance to the park is clearly marked where Falls Road bisects MacArthur Boulevard, although you'll have to pay $4 per carload to park near the tavern.

COURSE

The contrast between the downtown stretches of the C&O Towpath and the western sections of the trail is dramatic. This part of the towpath has a wild, almost primitive appeal, complete with gorges, rocky islands, and rushing white water. This 4.2-mile loop extends along the water and into the hills above the Potomac, with a variety of excellent options for extending the route.

The run starts just beyond the park entrance at Great Falls Tavern. An out-and-back dash on the towpath is the easiest option, but there's also a fine network of trails in the woods above the path that adds extra distance and makes for an agreeable start. The main loop through the hills follows the Gold Mine Trail (blue dot), which you reach by a steep climb up Lock 19 loop (yellow dot) that runs for a half mile before you take a right to the Gold Mine Trail.

The trail levels out after you make the climb to the Gold Mine loop. Early in the loop there's a choice for the lower or upper section. The upper loop adds extra distance and runs past the entrance to the old Maryland Mine on the left, and it provides a brief glimpse of MacArthur Boulevard as you wind along the perimeter of the park.

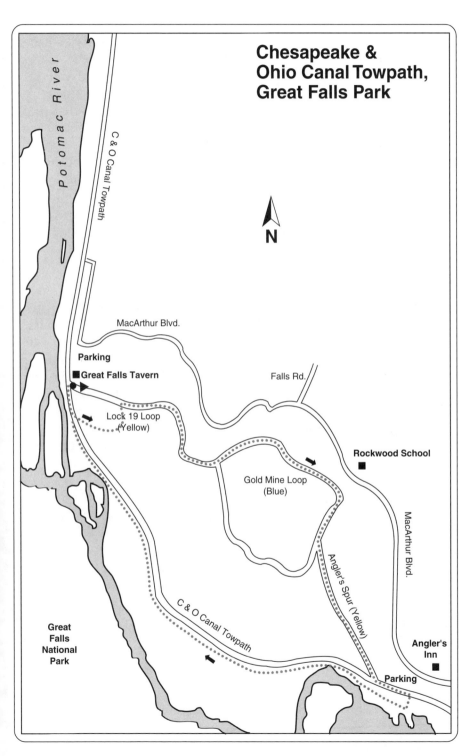

Chesapeake & Ohio Canal Towpath, Great Falls Park

Potomac River

C & O Canal Towpath

N

MacArthur Blvd.

Parking

■ Great Falls Tavern

Falls Rd.

Lock 19 Loop (Yellow)

Rockwood School ■

Gold Mine Loop (Blue)

MacArthur Blvd.

Angler's Spur (Yellow)

C & O Canal Towpath

Great Falls National Park

Angler's Inn ■

Parking

A left onto the half-mile-long Angler's Spur Trail (gold dot) closes the first half of the run with a downhill stretch to Berma Road—be sure to avoid the left for the Rockwood School that appears just before Angler's Spur. Berma Road is a secluded dirt road marked by a chain-link fence that runs parallel to the towpath. Take a left at the fence and follow the detour signs back to the towpath, which you'll pick up just shy of the Angler's Inn.

The run back on the towpath offers a fine contrast to the woods trails on the way out, with a tunnel-like stretch through a gorge, and with headwinds that can be brutal in the winter or welcome in the summer. This stretch of the Potomac contains plenty of white water, especially at the beginning and the end of the route. The only tricky stretch is a rocky section just short of the Lock 17 footbridge.

EXTENSIONS AND OPTIONS

The simplest way to add distance to this run is to use one of the many trails through the woods in the hills above the river, almost all of which are well marked and easy to run on, albeit somewhat challenging. For the chronically underchallenged with a penchant for rock climbing, another option on the way back is the 2-mile Billy Goat Trail that runs right along the water. Be forewarned, however, that this craggy trail more than lives up to its moniker, at times resembling a marine fitness course more than a running trail.

Finally, for those in search of a long run, an easy way to double the distance is to go 2 more miles on the towpath to Carderock.

PRINCE WILLIAM FOREST

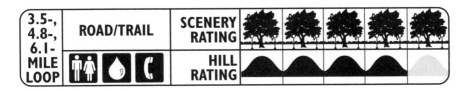

ACCESS

Prince William Forest is approximately 30 miles southwest of downtown Washington. Follow Route 95 from either the Beltway or the downtown area until you reach exit 150B. The park entrance is just to the right after you come to the exit. There's a $4 entrance fee at the gate; continue for approximately 2 miles until you reach the Visitor Center. Make sure you pick up a map at either the front gate or the Visitor Center.

All three runs begin from parking lot H, which you can reach from the Visitor Center by way of Scenic Drive. Take the left at the signs for Turkey Run, then go past the entrance for Turkey Run and follow the alphabetically labeled lots until you come to lot H. Be aware that this is a skewed alphabet in which, for some reason, lot I comes *before* lot H.

COURSE

These three runs offer the best of all possible worlds when it comes to trail running—a choice of distances, tough but suitably brief stretches of hilly terrain, and lots of deep woods filled with wildlife. It's a bit of a drive to get here and the $4 charge is steep, but the range of choices when it comes to trails and terrain makes it worth the trip.

All three runs start from lot H in the middle of Prince William Forest, a 17,000-acre watershed at the edge of the Piedmont Forest that drains to Chesapeake Bay. Most of the run takes you along narrow woods trails, but there's also a brief stretch of road running as well as a wide, easy-to-negotiate fire-road trail. The three runs are contiguous, and each is well marked and easy to follow. The short run is described first, followed by the two longer runs, which share much terrain.

SHORT LOOP (3.5 MILES)

If you run this loop clockwise from the parking lot, you'll start in the woods and finish on the road via Scenic Drive. If you run counterclockwise, you get to finish in the woods, but you'll have to negotiate a fairly tough climb at the end. For simplicity, this description assumes a start in the woods from the High Meadows Trail.

Cross the road from the lot and pick up the orange blazes for the High Meadows Trail, which runs for 0.8 miles before it bisects Taylor Road, a fire-road trail that leads to the South Valley Trail. The High Meadows Trail is the toughest part of the run, but the climb at the beginning is balanced by an enjoyable downhill stretch before you take a pair of rights, one to Taylor Road and the next to the South Valley Trail, which is marked by white blazes.

This trail, which follows the South Fork of Quantico Creek (the park is located northeast of the Quantico Marine Base), remains fairly level close to the water, but there are some tough, short hills when it climbs back from the creek. You'll cross the creek twice, once at the beginning shortly after you enter the trail (the water will be on your right after you cross), then again after approximately a half mile when the creek widens into a pond that's used for swimming by summer campers who rent cabins near the creek.

After a mile on the South Valley Trail, you'll come to a small flight of steps that leads up to Malawi Road, a wide, gravel access road for the cabins. Take a right and follow Malawi uphill for just under a half mile to parking lot G. Take another right out of the lot onto Scenic Drive and run the final mile back to the start at parking lot H. Scenic Drive has relatively narrow shoulders but wide grassy borders on either side and little traffic most of the time.

LONG LOOPS (4.8 MILES AND 6.1 MILES)

Both of the longer loops start with the same stretch along the High Meadows Trail, but you don't have to choose your distance until you're well into the run. Take the right from High Meadows onto Taylor road, a fire road that comes to the white-blazed South Valley Trail after 0.7 miles.

After running for 1.3 miles on the South Valley Trail, you come to a fork that represents the decision point for either the 4.8- or the 6.1-mile route (a concrete trail marker signifies this split). If you're taking the shorter route, make a right and again pick up the orange blazes of the High Meadows Trail, where you'll have a tough but enjoyable 0.8 mile climb to get back to the parking lot.

If you're going the distance, stay straight on the South Valley Trail, which crosses the creek twice, once just after the fork and again after

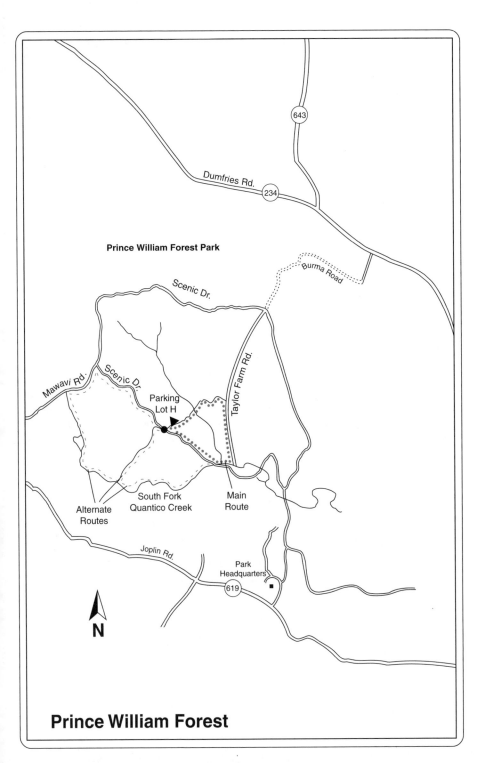

Prince William Forest Park

Prince William Forest

another half mile before the creek widens into a pond. A mile after the fork you'll come to Malawi Road, a wide, gravel access road that's used by campers to reach the cabins behind the creek. Follow Malawi for just under a half mile to parking lot G, then take a right and run the final mile on Scenic Drive (which offers wide grassy shoulders for fairly easy road running) back to parking lot H.

SAFETY ISSUES

This trail comes with its share of ticks, mosquitoes, and snakes in the summer, although the snakes are generally reticent to the point of invisibility. Mud, ice, and snow can be significant winter issues, although most of these trails dry out fairly quickly. If you're going for a long run it's not a bad idea to strap on a belt pack with water and first-aid equipment; it's easy to sprain an ankle here if you're not an experienced trail runner.

OTHER POSSIBILITIES

If tough trail running isn't your idea of a good time, the various fire roads are generally wide and accessible, and for road runners the 12-mile Scenic Drive is conveniently equipped with mile markers. Stop in at the Visitor Center and inquire about the book of measured loops the rangers keep at the front desk, or be creative and use the maps to invent your own route from the available combination of trails, fire roads, and road-running options.

SENECA CREEK STATE PARK

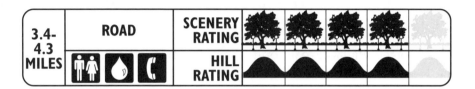

3.4-4.3 MILES	ROAD	SCENERY RATING	
	🚻 💧 ☎	HILL RATING	

ACCESS

Take I-270 north to the exit for Clopper Road west (Maryland Route 117), then drive for approximately 2 miles to the park entrance on the left. Stop at the Visitor Center to pick up a map of the park roads and trails. From there continue through the Contact Station (a small fee is collected in season) to a stop sign, then take a right and then the first left into the Pines Picnic Area playground parking lot.

COURSE

This route, a hilly road run through the woods and fields of Seneca Creek State Park, is a variation on the course used by the Montgomery County Road Runners Club for its Piece of Cake 10K and for the Turkey Burnoff 5-mile races.

The warm-weather attractions here include deer, a wide variety of birds, spring wildflowers, and some summer shade, and the activity list includes paddleboat rentals and a Frisbee golf course. In the winter, snow occasionally turns the park into a white wilderness with cross-country skiers dotting the woods and stretches of the shoreline along the lake.

The run starts at the north end of the Pines Picnic Area playground parking lot, where you'll take a left at the stop sign. The roads are open to auto traffic, so keep to the left and exercise caution. Along the main road you'll pass turnoffs for the Chickadee Picnic Area and the Kingfisher Overlook. Continue downhill and cross the earthen dam as you take in views of Clopper Lake just beyond the half-mile mark.

Approximately a mile later, turn left at the stop sign at the game field and pass the Quail Ridge Picnic Area. Then turn left at the "Do Not Enter" sign and run clockwise around the Deer Ridge Picnic Area loop (at this point you'll have run approximately 2 miles). Retrace your steps to the game field, turn right, and continue back to the playground parking lot for a 3.4-mile run.

To extend the run to 4.3 miles, continue straight on the main road. Take the next right at a stop sign and run clockwise around the Oriole and Pines Picnic areas to return to the playground parking lot on the left. There's a nice view of the lake at the turnoff for the boat rental center.

Besides the available road routes, Seneca Creek Park has a number of marked dirt paths that go through undeveloped sections of the park and offer challenging trail running. A trail map is available at the Visitor Center. If the weather is problematic, both inexperienced and veteran trail runners should consult a ranger regarding trail conditions.

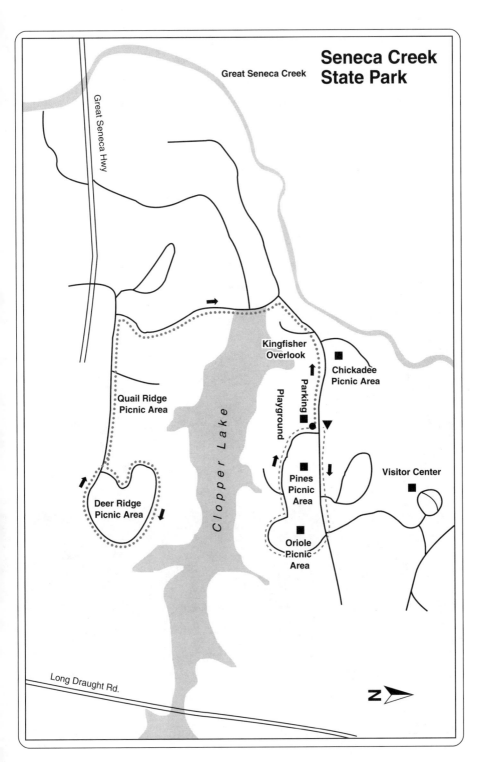

Seneca Creek State Park

ROAD RACES

1. Marine Corps Marathon
2. Cherry Blossom Ten-Mile Race
3. George Washington Parkway Classic 15K
4. Annapolis Run
5. Rockville Twilight 8K
6. Georgetown Classic 10K

MARINE CORPS MARATHON

26.2 MILES	ROAD	SCENERY RATING					
	LATE OCTOBER	HILL RATING					

In 1976, a group of marines got together to try to find a way to celebrate the 200th anniversary of the U.S. Marine Corps . . .

This may sound like the beginning of a fitness horror story, leading up to some physical challenge that combines the more torturous aspects of Outward Bound with the body-draining depletion of triathlons and ultramarathoning. But the marines who met that day chose a marathon as the event that would best test the determination, endurance, and strength that are integral to the Marine Corps credo.

What those marines had no way of knowing is that they were about to initiate the race that has become known as one of America's most personal marathons. Of the 15,000 or so runners who annually tackle the course, approximately half are first-timers. There are plenty of good reasons for that balance between novices and experienced marathoners. The marines who organize the race and serve as volunteers along the course have developed a reputation for the personal touch in supplying directions, first aid, hydration, and whatever else may be necessary to not only finish but enjoy the race.

There are also many reasons why the Marine Corps Marathon now competes with New York for the title of "The People's Marathon." New York may have once been a simple affair, but the vagaries of corporate sponsors, complex logistics, and the anxiety that outsiders feel at the prospect of going from borough to borough may have taken their toll. And Boston may have its history and the glorious suffering of Heartbreak Hill, but getting to Hopkinton on time can be a nightmare.

The Marine Corps Marathon, meanwhile, has been lauded for accessibility by everyone from *Runners World* to *The Ultimate Guide to Marathons*, which gave the event a rating of 99.2 out a possible 100—this despite being the fourth largest marathon in the country, behind only New York, Honolulu, and Los Angeles.

The Marine Corps Marathon also has a solid fallback option when it comes to catchy nicknames—"Marathon of the Monuments." The

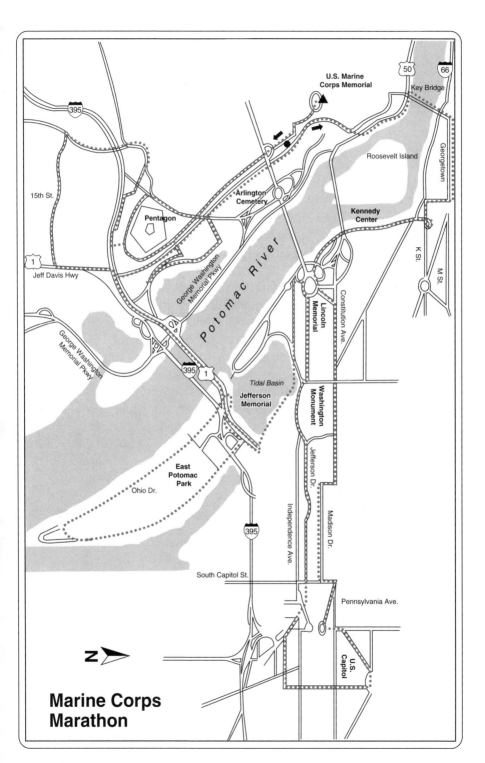

U.S. Marine
Corps Memorial

50

66

Key Bridge

395

Georgetown

Roosevelt Island

15th St.

Arlington
Cemetery

Pentagon

Kennedy
Center

K St.

M St.

1

Jeff Davis Hwy

George Washington
Memorial Pkwy

Potomac River

Lincoln
Memorial

Constitution Ave.

George Washington
Memorial Pkwy

395

1

Tidal Basin

Jefferson
Memorial

Washington
Monument

Jefferson Dr.

East
Potomac
Park

Ohio Dr.

Madison Dr.

Independence Ave.

395

South Capitol St.

Pennsylvania Ave.

U.S.
Capitol

N

**Marine Corps
Marathon**

guidebook for the event lists almost a dozen, the most obvious being the Marine Corps War Memorial (Iwo Jima Monument), along with the Vietnam Veterans Memorial and the Vietnam Women's Memorial.

The mostly flat course also passes by the *de rigueur* Washington tourist attractions, including the White House, the Washington Monument, the Lincoln and Jefferson Memorials, the Capitol, Arlington National Cemetery, the Pentagon, and the Kennedy Center.

The combination of friendly atmosphere, military precision in organization, and the absence of prize money tends to produce some unusual conditions, the first being an abundance of running teams from both military and civilian groups. The winning times tend to be a bit less startling and superhuman than usual, particularly for the men, with the first runner generally clocking in sometime shortly after the 2:15 mark.

Those truly desperate for marathon trivia may wish to be informed that Oprah Winfrey ran her first marathon here in 1994 with a final time of 4:29:15, placing her 8,210th out of 12,716 finishers. No word on what that time will transform to in the latest exercise video.

Washington weather also occasionally plays a significant part in the race. The late-October start generally ensures conditions that are close to optimal, but the occasional Indian-summer day can produce temperatures that are a bit too balmy for distance running, and the fall rains have been known to put a damper on the proceedings.

Finally, give the folks who run this race credit for showing steadfast military attention to detail. A typical guidebook for the Marine Corps Marathon reveals that the event required 60,000 safety pins, 400 Ace bandage rolls, 303,000 paper cups (always wondered about that, didn't you?), and 138 pounds of petroleum jelly to ease the pain from one of the few sources of friction in this well-run race.

CHERRY BLOSSOM TEN-MILE RACE

10 MILES	ROAD	SCENERY RATING					
	EARLY APRIL	HILL RATING					

Along with the lighting of the Japanese lanterns at the Tidal Basin and the White House Easter Egg Roll, the Cherry Blossom Ten-Mile race has been one of Washington's spring rituals for the last quarter century.

Held two weeks before the Boston Marathon on a fast, flat course that covers many of D.C.'s best tourist spots, the race has also become a prime warm-up for the Boston Marathon (the lure of big-bucks prize money doesn't hurt, either). Bill Rodgers, Greg Meyer, and Lisa Larsen all won in New England after coming in first here.

Originally christened the Cherry Blossom Invitational run, the race was conceived in 1973 by Gar Williams, president of the D.C. Road Runners Club, and Ralph Reynolds, program director of Washington's Central YMCA. The run coincides with the city's Cherry Blossom Festival, when blooming magnolias, forsythia, and cherry trees line the paths and roads along the Potomac.

The highlights of the course include Rock Creek Regional Park, the Kennedy Center, a stunning stretch across the Memorial Bridge into Arlington, and a section that runs along Independence Avenue and around the Tidal Basin. The course seems to change slightly on an almost annual basis to meet various Park Service requirements.

The field has grown from a humble total of 200 runners for the inaugural event to a lottery-controlled field of approximately 6,000. The competition has toughened as well—the recent rise of the Kenyans in the last decade has lowered the men's course record to under 46 minutes, and it will be only a matter of time until the women's course record begins to push the 50-minute mark, which has already fallen in the men's masters division.

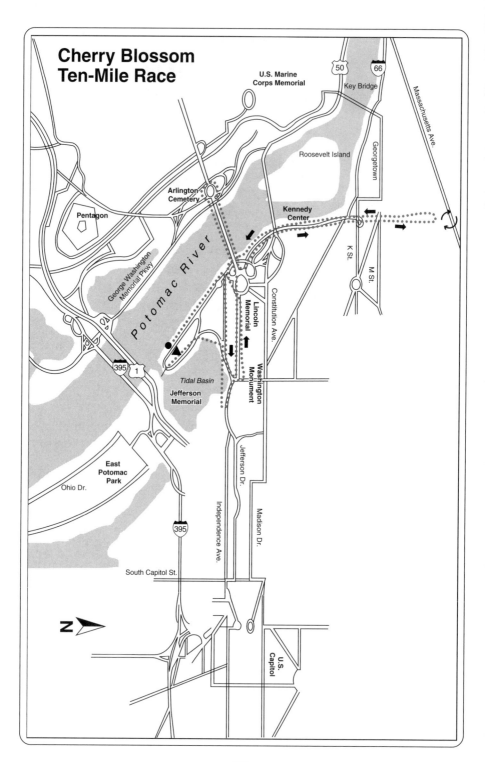

Cherry Blossom
Ten-Mile Race

U.S. Marine
Corps Memorial

Key Bridge

Roosevelt Island

Massachusetts Ave.

Georgetown

Arlington
Cemetery

Kennedy
Center

Pentagon

K St.

M St.

George Washington
Memorial Pkwy

Potomac River

Lincoln
Memorial

Constitution Ave.

Washington
Monument

Tidal Basin

Jefferson
Memorial

East
Potomac
Park

Ohio Dr.

Jefferson Dr.

Independence Ave.

Madison Dr.

South Capitol St.

U.S.
Capitol

N

GEORGE WASHINGTON PARKWAY CLASSIC 15K

9.3 MILES	ROAD	SCENERY RATING	🌲🌲🌲🌲🌲
	MID-APRIL	HILL RATING	⛰️⛰️⛰️

For 364 days a year, Washington runners meander up and down the Potomac and Chesapeake Bay on the lovely Mount Vernon Trail, putting up with a small amount of nuisance traffic from the nearby George Washington Parkway, which runs parallel with the trail for most of its length. Then, for one (hopefully) pristine day in April, they get to be the traffic, commandeering the length of the parkway in this road race from Mount Vernon to Alexandria.

While the idea of a parkway classic may seem like an oxymoron, it's hard to dispute the PR blurb that modestly declares this race to be "one of the ten most scenic footraces in the country."

As for the course, the beauty of the parkway speaks for itself. It was built in 1929 to showcase the area, and while some of the terrain has absorbed its share of "malling," the cleared roadway itself is a pleasure to run on. The combination of a downhill course and a full complement of blooming Washington greenery makes this one a genuine attraction.

The course begins at the Mount Vernon home of George Washington (see "Southern Mount Vernon Trail" in "Parks and Paths"), then breaks east toward Fort Hunt Park. It passes the scenic Belle Haven Picnic area just after the 7-mile mark, then hooks back through Alexandria to finish at Jones Point Park. The course is over gently rolling terrain with an overall downhill—the course peaks out at 95 feet, then finishes at just 8 feet above sea level.

The race also features some decent competition. It's not uncommon for either the male or female winner of the most recent Marine Corps Marathon to show up, and several recent runnings have featured a highly competitive contingent of Russian runners. Few Kenyans have been sighted as of this writing, so this is still a competitive race in the truest sense of the word.

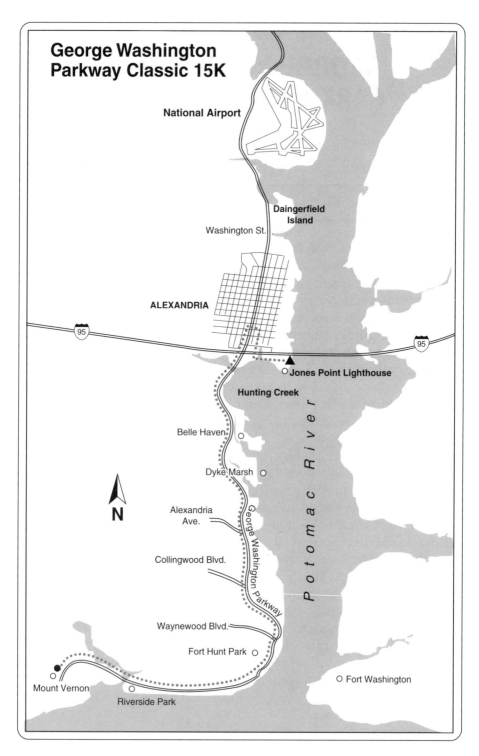

George Washington Parkway Classic 15K

National Airport

Daingerfield Island

Washington St.

ALEXANDRIA

95

95

Jones Point Lighthouse

Hunting Creek

Belle Haven

Dyke Marsh

Alexandria Ave.

Collingwood Blvd.

George Washington Parkway

Potomac River

N

Waynewood Blvd.

Fort Hunt Park

Mount Vernon

Fort Washington

Riverside Park

ANNAPOLIS RUN

10 MILES	ROAD	SCENERY RATING					
	LATE AUGUST	HILL RATING					

Although it might seem like a stretch to lump Annapolis into the Washington road-race scene, this 10-mile race has become a highlight of the local circuit. It's highly regarded well beyond the Beltway as well. It's considered Maryland's premier road race, and is rated one of the top 100 races in the country by *Runners World*.

Organized in 1975 by the Annapolis Striders, the course starts and finishes just outside the Navy–Marine Corps Memorial Stadium. The course is practically a guided historical tour of U.S. military education, cutting through West Annapolis after leaving the stadium, then crossing the Severn River to the shaded country roads and rolling hills of the Ritchie Highway before traversing a scenic stretch along the sea walls in the Naval Academy. The last section of the course features a tour through historic downtown Annapolis, past St. John's College, and the finish just outside the stadium (the awards ceremony itself is held in the stadium).

Historical considerations aside, this race makes its name from its reputation as one of the best-organized races in the country. The relative absence of big prize money keeps the competition level down a bit among those in the field, which usually averages between 2,000 and 3,000 runners, but a solid contingent of local runners and the military presence ensure a fairly impressive winning time.

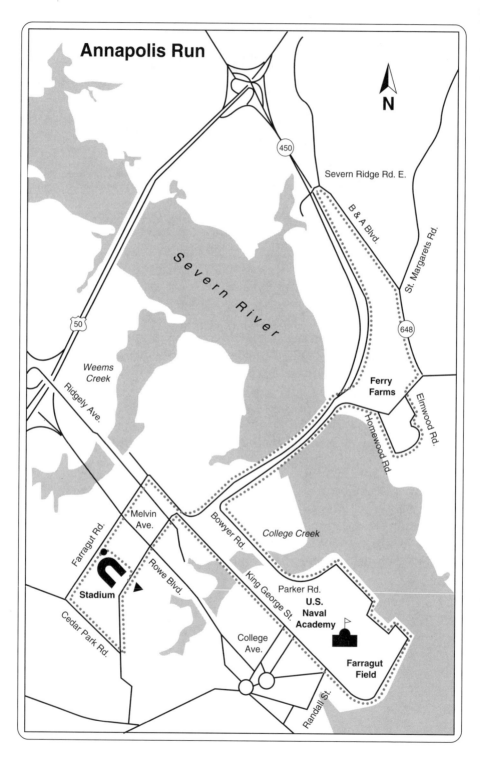

Annapolis Run

N

Severn River

Severn Ridge Rd. E.

B & A Blvd.

St. Margarets Rd.

450

648

Weems Creek

Ridgely Ave.

Ferry Farms

Elmwood Rd.

Homewood Rd.

50

Melvin Ave.

Bowyer Rd.

College Creek

Farragut Rd.

Rowe Blvd.

King George St.

Parker Rd.

U.S. Naval Academy

Stadium

Cedar Park Rd.

College Ave.

Farragut Field

Randall St.

ROCKVILLE TWILIGHT 8K

4.8 MILES	ROAD	SCENERY RATING					
	MID TO LATE JULY	HILL RATING					

Although summer road racing is generally considered anathema in the D.C. area because of the heat and humidity, one of the major pleasant exceptions is the Rockville Rotary Twilight Runfest, which features an 8K race and a 1K fun run. The race, which can be reached by Metro at the Rockville station, runs through downtown Rockville, a pleasant suburban town just beyond the Beltway northwest of Washington, D.C., in Montgomery County.

The highlight of the moderately hilly course is the stretch around the Montgomery County College campus before the return to Rockville center. Most of the course is pleasantly suburban in nature. The twilight start is unusual, often guaranteeing a colorful sunset as part of the initial backdrop, and a good part of the race takes place in the dark, which has a certain novelty appeal.

In keeping with the spirit of the season, this tends to be a laid-back run that functions more as an excuse for an old-fashioned town festival and community party. A runner's clinic is held during the race weekend, and the festival that precedes the evening start features a good live band. The reasonably short distance is enough to get a good workout and fuel the competitive fires of those capable of standing up to the humidity, but most runners are primarily grateful for the chance for a good time and the extra attention to seasonal considerations.

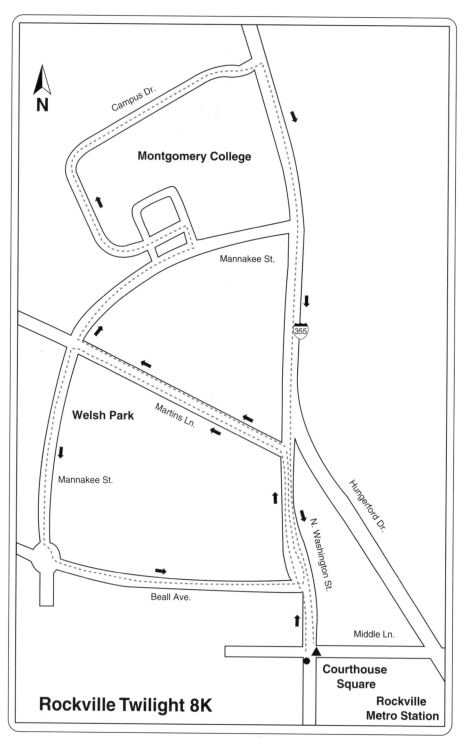

N

Campus Dr.

Montgomery College

Mannakee St.

355

Welsh Park

Martins Ln.

Mannakee St.

Hungerford Dr.

N. Washington St.

Beall Ave.

Middle Ln.

Courthouse Square

Rockville Metro Station

Rockville Twilight 8K

GEORGETOWN CLASSIC 10K

6.2 MILES	ROAD	SCENERY RATING	
	EARLY OCTOBER	HILL RATING	

Long known for its challenging hills and tour of historic Georgetown, the Georgetown Classic 10K is an important stop on the Washington, D.C., fall racing circuit. The race is positioned to be a test of runners' conditioning and training for the Marine Corps Marathon, just three weeks later.

Begun in 1980 with fewer than 300 runners, the race has grown to 3,600. For most of the first 17 years of the race, the course remained the same, with only minor adjustments to eliminate the cobblestone streets in Georgetown. In 1997, the course was redesigned to eliminate the worst of the hills and to reduce the impact on Wisconsin Avenue, a major artery through Georgetown.

From its start on M Street, near the Key Bridge, the course runs levelly along Canal Road for 2 miles before climbing hills into the residential neighborhoods up from the Potomac River. The worst of the hills, on Garfield Street, is known as "Mt. Garfield"; here, even some of the 7-8 minutes-per-mile runners are reduced to walking. After cresting the hill at about 3.5 miles, the course rolls until the last 1.6-mile net downhill stretch to the end on M Street, creating a very fast finish. Starting in 1998, this is one of the first area races to use the ChampionChip race timing system, giving runners both "clock" and "net" times.

After meeting the challenge of the Georgetown hills, runners celebrate their accomplishment and enjoy a guiltless post-race Street Festival featuring hot food, cold beer, live music, and other activities. The race has a generous awards structure, offering over $2,500 in gift certificates. Prizes are awarded for the top ten overall, for the top three in five-year age groups up to 75 and above, and for numerous random prizes.

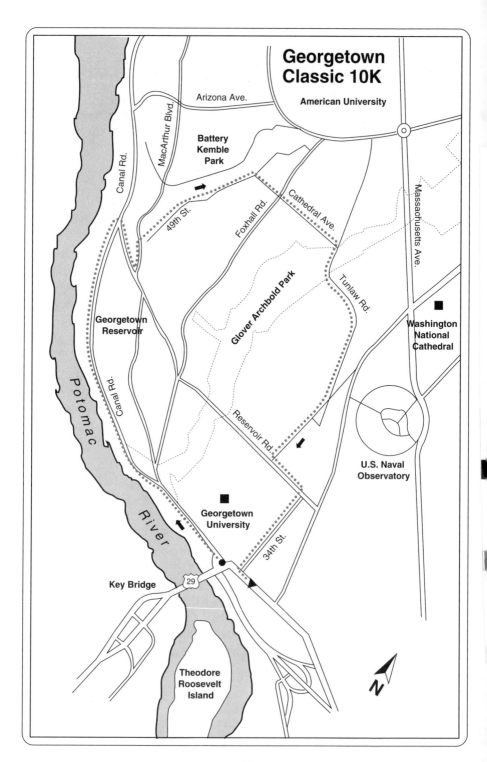

Georgetown
Classic 10K

APPENDIX

The Washington, D.C., area has running clubs ranging from small groups that get together for weekend runs or to train competitively to large organizations that have programs for runners of all ages and abilities. We've listed the running clubs in the greater Washington, D.C., metropolitan area affiliated with the Road Runners Club of America (RRCA). They provide a large variety of running-related activities, including regularly scheduled long runs, track workouts, training programs, and races. All of these clubs have excellent Web sites that provide comprehensive information on their activities.

Washington, D.C.

RRCA clubs in the immediate Washington, D.C., metropolitan area:

Montgomery County Road Runners Club
P.O. Box 1703
Rockville, Maryland 20849
Web: http://www.mcrrc.org

D.C. Road Runners Club
P.O. Box 1352
Arlington, Virginia 22201
Web: http://www.patriot.net/users/dcrrc

Northern Virginia Running Club (NOVA)
130 N. Payne Street
Alexandria, Virginia 22314
Web: http://www.tiac.net/users/tumg/nova_runners

Virginia Happy Trails Running Club
8396 Idylwood Road
Vienna, Virginia 22182
Web: http://vhtrc.simplenet.com

Suburbs

RRCA clubs in Virginia in the Washington, D.C., region:

Reston Runners
P.O. Box 2924
Reston, Virginia 22090
Web: http://restonrunners.org

Prince William Running Club
P.O. Box 602
Garrisonville, Virginia 22463
Web: http://users.aol.com/pwrc

Fredericksburg Area Running Club
P.O. Box 3653
Fredericksburg, Virginia 22402
Web: http://www.farc.org

RRCA clubs in Maryland in the Washington, D.C., region:

Howard County Striders
P.O. Box 563
Columbia, Maryland 21045
Web: http://www.onlinesol.com/online/striders

Frederick Steeplechasers
P.O. Box 681
Frederick, Maryland 21705
Web: http://members.aol.com/fsrcweb

Annapolis Striders
P.O. Box 187
Annapolis, Maryland 21404
Web: http://www.annapolisstriders.home.ml.org

The Washington area is also the hometown of the national office of the Road Runners Club of America, providing support for grassroots running throughout the country. You can obtain a wide variety of running-related information (local and national) by visiting or writing the RRCA at its Alexandria office, or from its Web site.

Road Runners Club of America
1150 S. Washington St., Suite 250
Alexandria, Virginia 22314
Web: http://www.rrca.org

OTHER BOOKS IN THE RUNNING GUIDE SERIES

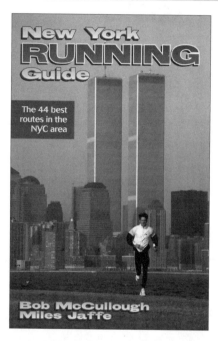

The 44 best routes in the NYC area

Bob McCullough
Miles Jaffe

The 45 best routes in the Bay Area

Bob Cooper

Now, with the *New York Running Guide*, finding great places to run in the Big Apple is easy. You'll find all the information you need to enjoy 44 of the best routes throughout New York's five boroughs, Long Island, and New Jersey. Eight of the routes in the book are profiles of the best races in the New York City area. Experience the best of New York City while in your running shoes.

Item PMCC0765 • ISBN 0-88011-765-6
$16.95 ($24.95 Canadian)

San Francisco Running Guide simplifies runners' decision-making by providing detailed descriptions and maps of 35 of the Bay Area's best running routes and 10 of its major races. For each route, you're given a map and a route description, plus information on route distance, scenery, terrain, hill ratings, available facilities, and more. Experience firsthand the unique beauty of San Francisco and the Bay Area.

Item PCOO0703 • ISBN 0-88011-703-6
$16.95 ($24.95 Canadian)

HUMAN KINETICS
The Premier Publisher for Sports & Fitness
TO ORDER CALL 1-800-747-4457 (U.S.)
1-800-465-7301 (CANADA) • 217-351-5076 (INT'L)
www.humankinetics.com

2335

ABOUT THE AUTHORS

Don Carter has logged nearly 30,000 running miles in Washington, D.C., since moving to the area in 1980. He's also competed in over 200 races, including 30 major marathons. A past president of the Montgomery County Road Runners Club, the largest running club in the Washington, D.C., metro area, Carter has been an active promoter and organizer of running programs for the entire community. He has also written articles for his running club's newsletter, *The Rundown*, and for *FootNotes*. He currently resides in Alexandria, Virginia.

Robert McCullough is a journalist and author who lives near Boston, Massachusetts. He is also the author of a sports interview collection entitled *My Greatest Day in Baseball*, and his writing has appeared in the *Boston Globe*, the *Boston Phoenix*, the *Los Angeles Times*, *SPORT* Magazine, and the *New Age Journal*. He has run four marathons, including Boston twice, both times as a bandit.